I0815723

DreamWorks

DRAGONS

RECIPES FROM THE ISLE OF BERK

RECIPES FROM THE ISLE OF BERK

A Book of Feasts, Drinks, Desserts . . . and Dragons

Written by Fishlegs Ingerman

Foreword by Chief Hiccup Horrendous Haddock III

Translated from Old Norse by Daytona Danielsen and Erik Burnham

INSIGHT EDITIONS

SAN RAFAEL • LOS ANGELES • LONDON

CONTENTS

CHAPTER FOUR

FEASTS (MAIN DISHES)

CHAPTER FIVE

GROG (DRINKS)

CHAPTER SIX

DESSERTS

Recipes inspired by Mead Hall, Spit Fyre Grill, and Hooligan's Grog & Gruel in Isle of Berk at Universal Epic Universe

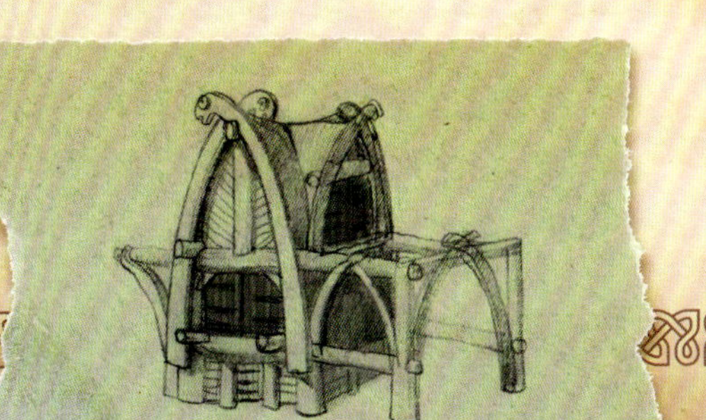

FOREWORD

This . . . is a cookbook.

It's full of our village's favorite foods. It's got grog and gruel and desserts, of course. Everything you could want for a Viking feast. In a word: delicious.

Every village cookbook has recipes, though. What makes ours different? Our recipes can be made hand in claw with fire. Dragon fire.

My name is Hiccup Horrendous Haddock III. (Great name, I know.) I'm the chief of Berk, a rough and rugged island that's twelve days north of hopeless and a few degrees south of freezing to death. It might snow nine months of the year and hail the other three (and that's if we have a mild year).

But Berk is so much more than what outsiders realize. It has something other places don't: sheep that stare directly into the depths of your soul. Wait, no. It's dragons. We have dragons! Lots of 'em! And they've changed everything for the better!

Once, everything about Berk was as tough as our weather. Our food? Tough and bland. Our sense of style? Drab and dull . . . But since we made peace with the dragons (which only took us 300 years) and became the world's first dragon-Viking utopia, life hasn't been the same.

Now the locals are colorful. And our cuisine has some actual flavor. A little spice, even! And we owe that to the inspiration we get from living around our dragon buds.

Living with dragons—it ain't easy. It's unpredictable. Risky. You need to be calm. Patient. Have a cool head. Not always easy with Vikings. But dragon training brings a new adventure—and a new dragon-inspired cooking method—every day.

Which brings me to this book. For generations, Vikings were at odds with dragons. But now we ride them. Live with them. They even help us with our daily chores, like cooking and cleaning (it's amazing how handy a burst of instant dragon fire can be).

My father always taught me that it's the responsibility of the chief—you might say the *chief responsibility*—to make sure everyone on Berk is taken care of. As we continue to merge our lifestyle with the dragons', one of the ways I'm going to do that is by making sure that the dragon-inspired cooking methods we've learned are available to everyone.

And no one is better suited for the job than my best friend, Fishlegs Ingerman—Log Master of our *Book of Dragons*. Since we've integrated dragons into our society, he's kept a detailed record of their every statistic and characteristic. And now he's collected our village's favorite recipes (and a few dragon facts) in one book.

You might be asking: Why include dragons? Why not just the recipes? Simple. When something changes your life for the better, you include it in your life as much as possible—from Dragon Races to exploring new worlds to helping cook meals in the longhouse.

It's the Berkian way!

Chief Hiccup Horrendous Haddock III

INTRODUCTION

Hello. This is Fishlegs Ingerman.

I'm a Dragon Rider and the keeper of dragon lore here on Berk. When Bork the Bold, the great-great-great grandfather of Gobber the Belch, wrote the original Book of Dragons, he kept a detailed record of his thoughts, feelings, and fears about dragons—he even wrote down lists of the foods he most liked to snack on when he was observing dragons in the wild! (Bork was very thorough, if not always entirely accurate.)

The proudest achievement of my life was to add to the Book of Dragons with new and more accurate information. I think that's part of the reason Chief Hiccup asked me to both follow Bork's lead and turn my attention to other chronicles, starting with this official collection of Berkian recipes and dragon-inspired cooking methods. (Cooking with dragon fire is a lot like cooking with any other kind of fire, but it's so much easier to start a fire when all you have to do is say "please" and offer a treat!)

During my research, I've found that if you wanna gain a dragon's trust, to befriend and train them, it's a great idea to feed them (just don't ever use eel!). I have also learned the hard way that you shouldn't rely on dragons alone to protect yourself. And you also shouldn't only rely on dragons to cook your food, so even though I've added dragon-inspired cooking methods to some recipes, most also include more conventional cooking techniques for when your Gronckle decides her sleep is more important than your sustenance. (It's okay though. Meatlug is so cute when she naps!)

In any case, this volume includes the foods that most regularly find their way to the village tables. Some of my favorites include Meatlug's Sweet Chocolate and Cherry Buns (page 26), Terrible Terror's Dilled Prawns (page 92), and Bewilderbeast's Icy Skyr (page 108)!

And what's better entertainment to accompany your meal than some dragon facts and observations?

To give you a sense of the value of each recipe, I've also rated entries with the Ingerman Classification System, the most advanced system on Berk (that doesn't require the use of sheep). I know that you'll find that as important and useful as I do.

Enjoy!

COOKING WITH FIRE

(WHEN YOU DON'T HAVE YOUR OWN DRAGON TO HELP YOU)

by Fishlegs Ingerman

I've spent a lot of time studying our dragon friends, and I've recently been captivated with finding out how each class is best utilized in the kitchen. My most important finding: We must prepare for the times when our dragon friends aren't in the mood to help with our feasts (which is basically always).

So, I've created a simple guide to different dragon-inspired cooking methods that each Berkian can refer to when cooking with dragon fire is not an option:

CLASS: BAKE AND ROAST

Think of baking and roasting almost like incubating a dragon egg—you need a stable heat source and the right conditions, and in the case of baking and roasting, it's a dry environment like an oven. The biggest difference between the two techniques is temperature, with baking generally lower than roasting. In many recipes, the terms might be virtually interchangeable, with baking being associated with, well, baked goods like cakes and pastries, and roasting associated with meats and vegetables. Here are ways to give each of these a try, along with some related "extra credit" techniques:

BAKING

- Ruffnut and Tuffnut's Nutty Granola with Skyr, Two Ways (page 21)
- Meatlug's Sweet Chocolate and Cherry Buns (page 26)
- Tuffnut's Braided Beard Bread (page 29)
- Chieftain's Cheese Pie (for Stoick the Vast) (page 31)
- Hiccup's Endive Bites with Cheese and Cured Meat (page 61)
- Stoick's Rustic Baked Meatballs with Honey Gravy and Geitost (page 87)
- Fishlegs's Fish Sticks with New Potatoes and Dill (page 95)
- Northern Lights Meringue Cake (page 118)
- For the Dancing and the Dreaming Rustic Layer Cake with Cream and Berries (page 121)
- Twelve Days North of Hopelessness Cake (page 122)

Each ring in this kransekake is individually baked and stacked to create this eye-catching cake.

- Hidden World Cookies (page 127)
- Gothi's Crest Cookies (page 128)
- Raincutter's Claws (page 134)
- Baked Apples with Rye and Vanilla Frozen Yogurt (page 139)
- Pepparkakor for Snoggletog (page 141)
- Berk Birkes (page 142)
- Skillet Apple Cake (page 145)

ROASTING

- Honey- and Lingonberry-Roasted Carrots (page 64)
- Zesty Cipollini Onions (pag 65)
- Balsamic Mushrooms (page 67)

- Sweet Potato Hash (page 68)
- Gobber the Belch's Roast Chicken with Beets and BBQ Sauce (page 76)

I don't know what's better: roasting this chicken in a simple iron pan or over an open flame with Gobber's rotisserie arm attachment.

- Stoick's Roast Pork with Vinegary Red Cabbage (Rødkål) and Apples (page 88)
- Gobber the Belch's Roasted Turkey Wings (page 84)
- Hiccup's Salmon with Potatoes (page 96)
- Whole Salt-Crust Roasted Fish (page 99)

EMBER ROASTING

- Potatoes with Charred Herbs (page 71)

TOASTING

- Raincutter's Rugbrød and Grubs (page 58)

CLASS: BRAISE, BOIL, AND SIMMER

The key to all of these is liquid—and not just in hot springs or lakes of lava—and a good pot. Braising is a fancy way of describing an otherwise simple process of slowly cooking meat or vegetables in a covered pot with a small amount of liquid, making even tougher meats tender. Simmering and boiling, on the other hand, generally submerge the food in a liquid like broth or water. Bonus points for trying poaching (which takes a simmer down a notch, allowing you to cook things like fish at a slow temperature while infusing it with all the good flavors of an aromatic poaching liquid) and scalding (which means bringing milk or cream to just below the boiling point).

BRAISING

- Stoick's Roast Pork with Vinegary Red Cabbage (Rødkål) and Apples (page 88)
- Astrid's Sausage over Sour Cabbage (Surkål) with Mustard (page 79)
- Dragon Fire Chicken Spire (page 82)

SIMMERING AND BOILING

- Hiccup's Harmless Porridge with Berries and Butter (page 18)
- Rhubarb-and-Berry Sour Candies (page 136)

POACHING

- Hiccup's Creamy Dill-Poached Haddock with New Potatoes (page 91)

Hiccup's secret to the perfect poached haddock: use milk instead of water!

SCALDING

- Tuffnut's Braided Beard Bread (page 29)

STEEPING

- Hiccup and Toothless's Smoky Strawberry Black Tea Blend (page 107)

CLASS: PAN-FRY, PAN-SEAR, SAUTÉ

These three simple techniques look similar but provide a range of results. Pan-frying food such as eggs at medium to high heat in oil or other fat, flipping it over midway to finish, will yield food that's cooked evenly on both sides, whereas pan-searing at high heat with oil will seal in juices (think fish or steak) and create a golden or brown surface but not with the intent of cooking the food through. Sautéing is similar to these, but you'll be tossing or stirring the ingredients (such as chopped onions, sliced mushrooms, etc.) in the pan.

PAN-FRYING

- Flaky Pan-Seared Cod with Potatoes, Creamed Greens, and Dill (page 89)

SAUTÉING

- Berkian Creamy Cod and Potato Stew (page 36)
- Gobber's Homemade Yak Noodle Soup (page 42)
- Raincutter's Rugbrød and Grubs (page 58)

CLASS: MELT, DOUBLE BOIL, DISSOLVE

Whether you're melting butter, creating a luscious cheese sauce, or dissolving honey in water on a stove at a low temperature, these generally gentle techniques are easy ways to get the littlest Dragon Riders-in-training involved in cooking (with adult supervision, of course).

MELTING

- Dragon Fire Chicken Spire (page 82)
- Raincutter's Claws (page 134)

DOUBLE BOIL

- Meatlug's Sweet Chocolate and Cherry Buns (page 26)

DISSOLVING

- Stoick's Homemade Bubbly Almost-Mead (page 115)

TEMPERING

- Plasma Blast Crème Brûlée with Berries (page 125)
- Honey-Vanilla Ice Cream (page 130)

The combination of potassium chloride and sugar in this dish creates a purple flame just like a Night Fury's plasma blast!

CLASS: NO FIRE REQUIRED (GREAT FOR BEWILDERBEAST RIDERS)

Don't tell the dragons, but it's possible to feed your crew mouthwatering dishes without heat. From creamy and fresh salads to a velvety cured salmon, keep these recipes on hand when the temperatures outside are sweltering or you're just looking for ease after a long day of riding.

NO-COOK EASE

- Valka's Creamy Cucumber and Fennel Salad with Skyr and Dill (page 44)
- Stormfly Slaw (page 47)
- Horseradish Crème (page 52)
- Horseradish Dill Crème Fraîche (page 53)
- Calabrian Chimi (page 56)
- Dill Fennel Chimi (page 57)
- Snaptrapper-Scented Chocolate-Berry Oat Bites (page 131)

- Bewilderbeast's Icy Skyr (page 108)
- Barf and Belch's Sweet-and-Sour Sea Buckthorn Smoothie (page 112)

CURING

- Isle of Gravlax (page 63)

Proper gravlax takes time, but there's nothing quite like it.

CLASS: MARINATE AND GRILL

These techniques go hand in hand. Marinating meat uses enzymes to break down proteins, like dragons' acidic saliva might, which then results in tender, flavorful food when it's later cooked on a grill.

MARINATING

- Spitfyre Steak Bowl (page 81)

GRILLING

- Spitfyre Steak Bowl (page 81)

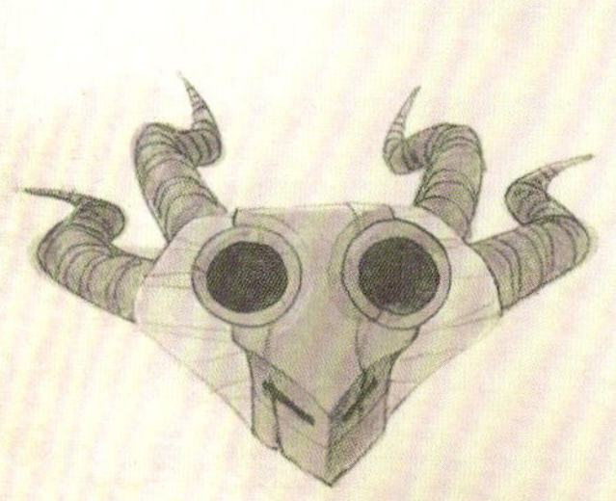

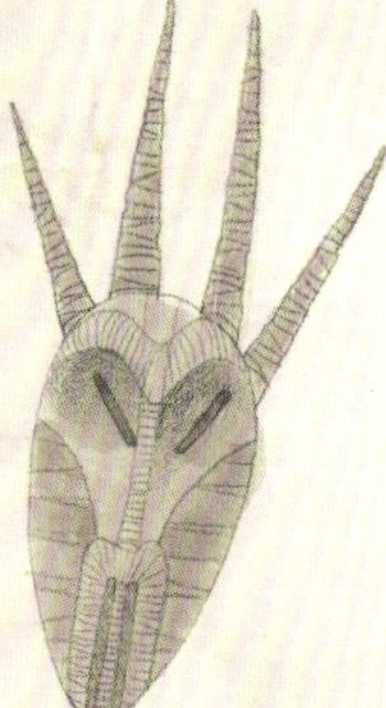

CLASS: TORCH AND FLAMBÉ

For Dragon Riders with a flair for fire and drama, a kitchen torch creates a controlled, direct flame, which easily caramelizes sugar. Flambéing requires a small amount of alcohol, which will ignite and then burn off, leaving an essence in its wake.

KITCHEN TORCH

- Hiccup's Harmless Porridge with Berries and Butter (page 18)
- Plasma Blast Crème Brûlée with Berries (page 125)

FLAMBÉ

- Fire and Honey Bacon (page 30)

RECOMMENDED TOOLS

Get the dragons to forge some new tools for you if you need them—cast-iron pans, cauldrons, and especially a heart-shaped waffle maker for Toothless's Treat Waffles (page 24), as well as a griddle for Sveler Shields (page 23) and Cloudjumper's Dragon-Wing Lefse (page 133)!

A NOTE FROM THE CHIEF ON GRUEL (AND OTHER WAYS TO BREAK FAST)

Once, and not so long ago, we Berkians didn't put quite so much thought into the first meal of the day. Nighttime feasting, however; now, that was what we were all about. But we noticed something about the eating habits of dragons since they came to Berk—not the part where they could swallow their whole meal in one gulp if they wanted to, though I admit, that was pretty impressive (and scary!).

No, we noticed that the dragons who ate first thing in the morning had a little more pep in their step than the ones who didn't . . . and after a little bit of experimentation, we learned that the same thing applied to humans, too.

For myself, I kind of like a nice bowl of Hiccup's Harmless Porridge with Berries and Butter (page 18)—but if gruel is an unusual punishment for you, there are some other breakfast possibilities in the next few pages, including Chieftain's Cheese Pie (for Stoick the Vast) (page 31) and some crowd-pleasing Fire and Honey Bacon (page 30).

—Hiccup Horrendous Haddock III

V+*, V, DF*, GF* | Serves 4

HICCUP'S HARMLESS PORRIDGE WITH BERRIES AND BUTTER

You know something Berk has a lot of, besides dragons, fish, and Vikings? Oats! That might be why porridge is as popular a breakfast as it is—most of us don't want to go against the grain, especially when it outnumbers us. (I didn't come up with that joke, Hiccup did. He loves a good bowl of porridge more than anyone.) If I had to guess, I'd say one reason that this porridge recipe is so popular on Berk is that smashing things can be fun—and this recipe lets you smash blueberries! (I suppose one might use a mortar and pestle if one doesn't have a spare Terrible Terror running around to help you with mashing.) Speaking of Terrible Terrors, one of them threw a tantrum and tried to burn Spitelout Jorgenson's porridge one day. Instead of burning it, it made a tasty little crust! You can get the same results with a nice little kitchen torch if your dragon decides to be stubborn—give it a try!

2½ cups water

1½ cups whole milk (see note)

1 cup steel-cut oats (see note)

¼ teaspoon Diamond Crystal kosher salt

¼ cup honey, plus more for serving (see note)

½ cup frozen blueberries, thawed

TIP: Fresh are okay here, too, but frozen break down more easily.

2 tablespoons granulated sugar, divided

2 tablespoons cold unsalted butter, in 4 thin slices

¼ cup hazelnuts, roughly chopped

Milk, cream, or dairy-free alternative, for serving

SPECIAL TOOLS

Mortar and pestle (optional)

Kitchen torch

In a medium or medium-large saucepan, pour in the water, milk, oats, and salt. Bring to a simmer over medium-high heat. Continue to cook, lowering the temperature to maintain a gentle simmer and stirring regularly so the oats don't stick to the bottom of the pan, for 25 to 30 minutes, or until the oats reach your ideal texture. (They'll continue to thicken as they cool.)

Remove from the heat and stir in the honey to sweeten. Add the blueberries, smashing them against the side of the pan with the back of a wooden spoon before swirling them into the porridge. (Alternatively, smash the blueberries in a small bowl or mortar and pestle.)

Divide between four bowls and scatter a thin, even layer of sugar over each. Ignite a kitchen torch. Holding it about 4 inches from the surface, circle it around the sugared surface until the sugar melts and solidifies into a crust. Repeat for the rest of the porridges. Add a slice of butter to the side of each serving, scatter hazelnuts next to each slice, drizzle honey over the top, and pour milk or cream around the rest of the edges to your taste. Then use a spoon to break the sugar crust, mix everything together, and chow down.

*NOTE: This recipe can be easily made dairy-free by substituting dairy-free alternatives, such as almond or coconut milk and plant-based butter, for the milk and butter. Easily make it vegan by substituting brown sugar for the honey and plant-based alternatives for the dairy products. Recipe is gluten free if you use certified gluten-free oats.

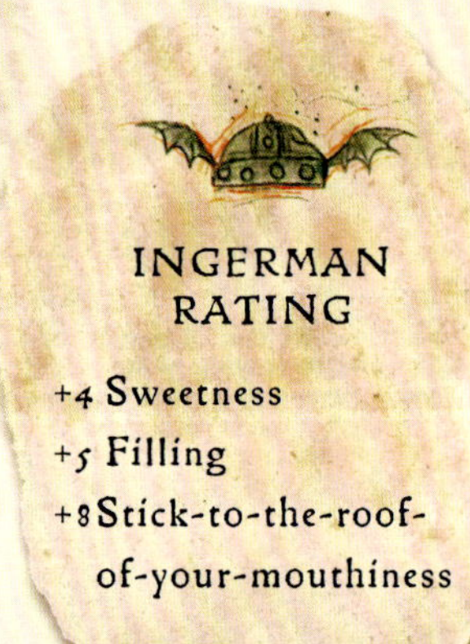

V+*, V, GF, DF* | Makes 8 cups granola

RUFFNUT AND TUFFNUT'S NUTTY GRANOLA WITH SKYR, TWO WAYS

The Hideous Zippleback is one dragon with two heads, two personalities, and two different moods that really has to work hard to get on the same page about anything. (Like a certain pair of twins I know.) Sometimes, with both Zipplebacks and people, the answer is to have multiple options coexisting together. A great way to do that for breakfast is this granola and skyr pairing. There are so many different combinations, even a Zippleback would be satisfied! Now, the best way to use a dragon to help prepare this breakfast is, of course, by toasting the granola nuts. But a Zippleback creates fire in a different way—with one head releasing a flammable gas and the other igniting it with a spark. The results are explosive! And maybe more than you need. If I were you, I'd use a good old-fashioned pan!

BASE

3 cups rolled oats (see note)

2 cups assorted seeds (a mix of sesame, chia, sunflower, and pepitas)

1 cup unsweetened coconut flakes

2 teaspoons vanilla extract

2 teaspoons ground cinnamon

1 teaspoon freshly ground cardamom

1 teaspoon sea salt

½ cup maple syrup

¼ cup coconut oil

RUFFNUT'S COMBO

½ cup chopped walnuts

½ cup chopped dried apples

Vanilla-flavored skyr, for serving (see note)

TUFFNUT'S COMBO

½ cup sliced almonds

½ cup dried blueberries

Blueberry-flavored skyr, for serving (see note)

Preheat the oven to 350°F and prep two large baking sheets by lining them with parchment paper.

TO MAKE THE BASE: In a large bowl, combine the oats, seeds, coconut flakes, vanilla, cinnamon, cardamom, and salt.

In a small saucepan over medium-low heat, heat the maple syrup and coconut oil until it's liquid (this should only take 30 seconds or so), then pour over the oat mixture. Stir to thoroughly coat, then divide the granola mix evenly between the two baking sheets. Add the walnuts to one baking sheet and the almonds to the other, mixing to coat, then spread the mix.

Bake, scraping and mixing occasionally, and rotating the sheets once, for about 16 minutes, then remove from the oven and turn off the heat.

TO MAKE RUFFNUT'S COMBO: To the granola containing walnuts, add the apples and stir to combine.

TO MAKE TUFFNUT'S COMBO: Add the dried blueberries to the other sheet and do the same. Let cool on the baking sheets.

Serve with skyr. Store leftovers in an airtight container.

*NOTE: Make certain that your chosen oats are processed in gluten-free facility to ensure this is a gluten-free meal. This recipe can also be made dairy-free or vegan by swapping out skyr for a preferred high-protein yogurt alternative.

HIDEOUS ZIPPLEBACK ABILITIES:

Flaming wheel-of-death

Barf: Ignites sparks

Belch: Emits flammable gas from its throat

INGERMAN RATING

+7 Creaminess

+3 Crispiness

+4 Variability

+4 Nuttiness

SVELER SHIELDS

There are two things that are important to any self-respecting Viking: shields, and an afternoon snack. Shields, of course, because the best offense is a good defense. You can't really be expected to fight bad guys like Drago Bludvist or Grimmel if you can't defend yourself! Whether it's from an unfriendly spear or a blast of flame from an untamed dragon, a shield is a must-have item. As far as afternoon snacks, there's nothing better than sveler—a thin pancake with just enough sweetness to give you some pep in your step. And do you know what else shields and sveler have in common? (Besides being round, Snotlout, I know how you think.) You can decorate them! Almost every Viking shield has a decoration on it, from a simple swirl or heraldric emblem to the bold colors that Astrid and Valka chose for theirs. Every sveler can be decorated, too, with a dragon portrait drawn in honey, maybe, or just a whole mess of fruit arranged in a pattern! Like we say when we're riding dragons—not even the sky is the limit!

INGERMAN RATING

+3 Sweetness

+9 Decorativeness

+10 Stackability

- 2 eggs
- ¾ cup granulated sugar
- 1½ cups buttermilk
- 1 teaspoon vanilla extract
- 2 cups all-purpose flour
- 1 teaspoon baking soda
- ⅛ teaspoon Diamond Crystal kosher salt
- Salted butter, for greasing
- Chocolate sauce or brown edible pen, for decorating
- Banana slices, for decorating
- 12 strawberry fans, for decorating
- Sliced almonds, for decorating
- Berry jams, for decorating
- Maple syrup, for serving (optional)

In a large mixing bowl, beat the eggs and sugar until smooth, then add the buttermilk and vanilla and stir to combine.

In another large bowl, sift together the flour, baking soda, and salt, then add to the eggs and beat until smooth and no lumps remain, taking care to not overmix. Let the batter rest for about 30 minutes.

Meanwhile, preheat a cast-iron frying pan (a regular pan will work, too) or pancake griddle over medium heat and grease with a little butter. Use a spoon or measuring cup to pour about 3 tablespoons of batter into the middle of the pan, evening it out with the back of a spoon if needed. Cook until bubbles start to appear on the surface or the underside is golden, about 1 minute, then flip with a spatula and cook the other side until golden and cooked through. Repeat with the remaining batter, buttering between sveler as needed.

Let each diner use the chocolate sauce or edible pen to draw the outline of the shield design on their sveler, then decorate with banana slices, strawberry fans, sliced almonds, and jam.

TIP: To create strawberry fans, create four or five slices from tip to nearly the stem without disconnecting them, then spread them out into a fan.

See page 151 for a template. Serve with maple syrup, if desired.

V | Makes about 12 waffles

TOOTHLESS'S TREAT WAFFLES

Night Fury dragons are possibly the rarest breed of dragon in existence (if there are any dragons rarer than that, I know I haven't seen them)! As such, our ability to learn anything about them didn't really start until Hiccup befriended Toothless. One of the most interesting things to me about Toothless—aside from his retractable teeth, which are just cool—is his notched tail fins. They're shaped just like a heart! Toothless was the first dragon to befriend a Viking on Berk—our chief, Hiccup—and we celebrate that in the best way we know how . . . with waffles. They can even be shaped to look like Toothless's tail! (Minus Hiccup's mechanical modifications, of course.)

- ½ cup (1 stick) salted butter, at room temperature
- 1 cup granulated sugar
- 4 eggs
- 1 cup buttermilk
- ½ cup whole milk
- 1 teaspoon vanilla extract
- 1 to 2 teaspoons blackberry extract
- 1¾ cups all-purpose flour
- ¼ cup Dutch-processed cocoa powder
- ½ teaspoon baking powder
- ½ teaspoon baking soda
- Black gel food coloring
- Red gel food coloring
- Whipped cream, for serving
- Fresh blackberries, for serving
- Fresh mint leaves, for garnish

SPECIAL TOOL

Heart-shaped waffle maker (see note)

In a large mixing bowl, cream the butter and sugar until fluffy. Add one egg at a time, mixing well—this will help the waffles become fluffy. Stir in the buttermilk, whole milk, and vanilla and blackberry extracts. Add the flour, cocoa powder, baking powder, and baking soda and mix to combine. Remove about a half cup of the batter and set aside. Add black gel food coloring to the main batter until the batter reaches the desired depth of black. Add red gel food coloring to the reserved section. Refrigerate for about a half an hour.

Preheat a heart-shaped waffle maker. Spoon a dollop of red batter at the base of one heart, then ladle a little less than a quarter cup of black batter (depending on the actual size of your waffle iron) onto the others and cook the waffles according to your model's instructions.

Serve with dollops of whipped cream and a scattering of fresh blackberries. Garnish with fresh mint leaves.

NOTE: The electric five-heart waffle makers that make Norwegian waffles are available online and at Scandinavian specialty stores. Look for ones that make five connected hearts at a time.

DRAGON STATS

TOOTHLESS

Species: Night Fury
Class: Strike
Attack: 15
Speed: 20
Armor: 18
Firepower: 14
Shot Limit: 6
Venom: 0
Jaw Strength: 6
Stealth: 18
Fire: Acetylen/oxygen-shaped plasma charges

MEATLUG'S SWEET CHOCOLATE AND CHERRY BUNS

Gronckles used to be one of the more feared species of dragons because they're super tough and highly maneuverable. Not many dragons can hover or fly backward, but a Gronckle can! They're fascinating creatures, but they're not just tough. In fact, ever since I've gotten to know Meatlug, all I can see is how sweet and gentle they can be. They have happy little eyes and big, adorable smiles, and they love nothing more than to snuggle (especially when they're babes)! Though Gronckles can have sweet natures, I don't think any of them could ever be sweeter than Meatlug. She's the most precious little Gronckle of them all! And this bun—plump and textured and so very sweet—it's so much like her, don't you think?

BUNS

- ½ cup (1 stick) salted butter
- 1¼ cups whole milk
- 2 tablespoons active dry yeast
- ¾ cup granulated sugar, divided
- 1 egg
- 1 teaspoon vanilla extract
- ½ teaspoon Diamond Crystal kosher salt
- 4½ cups all-purpose flour, divided, plus more as needed
- One 4-ounce milk chocolate baking bar, chopped
- ¾ cup dried cherries
- 2 tablespoons melted butter, for brushing

CHOCOLATE DRIZZLE

- One 4-ounce semisweet chocolate baking bar, chopped, for drizzling

SPECIAL TOOLS

- Bench scraper
- Double boiler (optional)

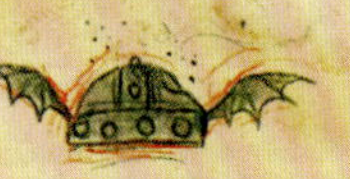

INGERMAN RATING

+8 Sweetness
+25 Reminiscence of Meatlug
+10 Portability

TO MAKE THE BUNS: In a small saucepan over medium heat, melt the butter. Add the milk and heat until it starts to bubble around the walls of the pot—this should take about 5 minutes or so—then remove from the heat and allow to cool until lukewarm.

Place the yeast and a tablespoon of the sugar in a large mixing bowl and pour ½ cup of the lukewarm milk into it, stirring briefly with a wooden spoon. Give it about 5 minutes for the yeast to bubble, then pour in the remaining milk and sugar. Then add the egg, vanilla, and salt.

Add half of the flour to the liquid and stir, then continue adding a half cup or so at a time until the dough is firm and releases from the sides of the bowl. At this point, lightly flour a clean working surface, turn the dough out onto this, and knead for about 10 minutes (see tip). Gather the dough into a ball.

TIP: Using a bench scraper makes kneading dough a foolproof—and stick-proof—process! To knead dough, dust a clean work surface such as a counter or pastry board with flour, then use your palms to press the dough down and push it away from you, letting it stretch and pull, then fold it over onto itself and rotate a quarter turn and repeat, generally about 10 minutes. Whenever it sticks to the surface, use the bench scraper to detach it and incorporate it to the main dough.

Wipe the mixing bowl you used earlier of excess dough (or use a new one) and lightly grease it. Return the ball of dough to the bowl and turn it to coat with the oil. Cover with a damp cloth and set it in a warm, draft-free place until it's doubled in size, about 1 hour.

Preheat the oven to 425°F and line two baking sheets with parchment. Punch down the dough, mix in the chopped milk chocolate bar and dried cherries, and divide the dough into 12 portions, forming each into a ball. Arrange these on the baking sheets, with the smoothest side up. Cover with damp towels to rise again, this time about 20 minutes. Brush with melted butter.

Working with one sheet at a time, bake in the center of the oven for about ten minutes, or until the buns are golden on top, rotating the baking sheet if needed for even baking. Cool on a wire rack.

TO MAKE THE CHOCOLATE DRIZZLE: Melt the semisweet baking bar in a double boiler or in the microwave (do this in a microwave-safe bowl, in 15-second intervals, stirring each time, until melted and smooth). Use a spoon to drizzle the chocolate in a zigzag over each of the buns. Let set, then serve.

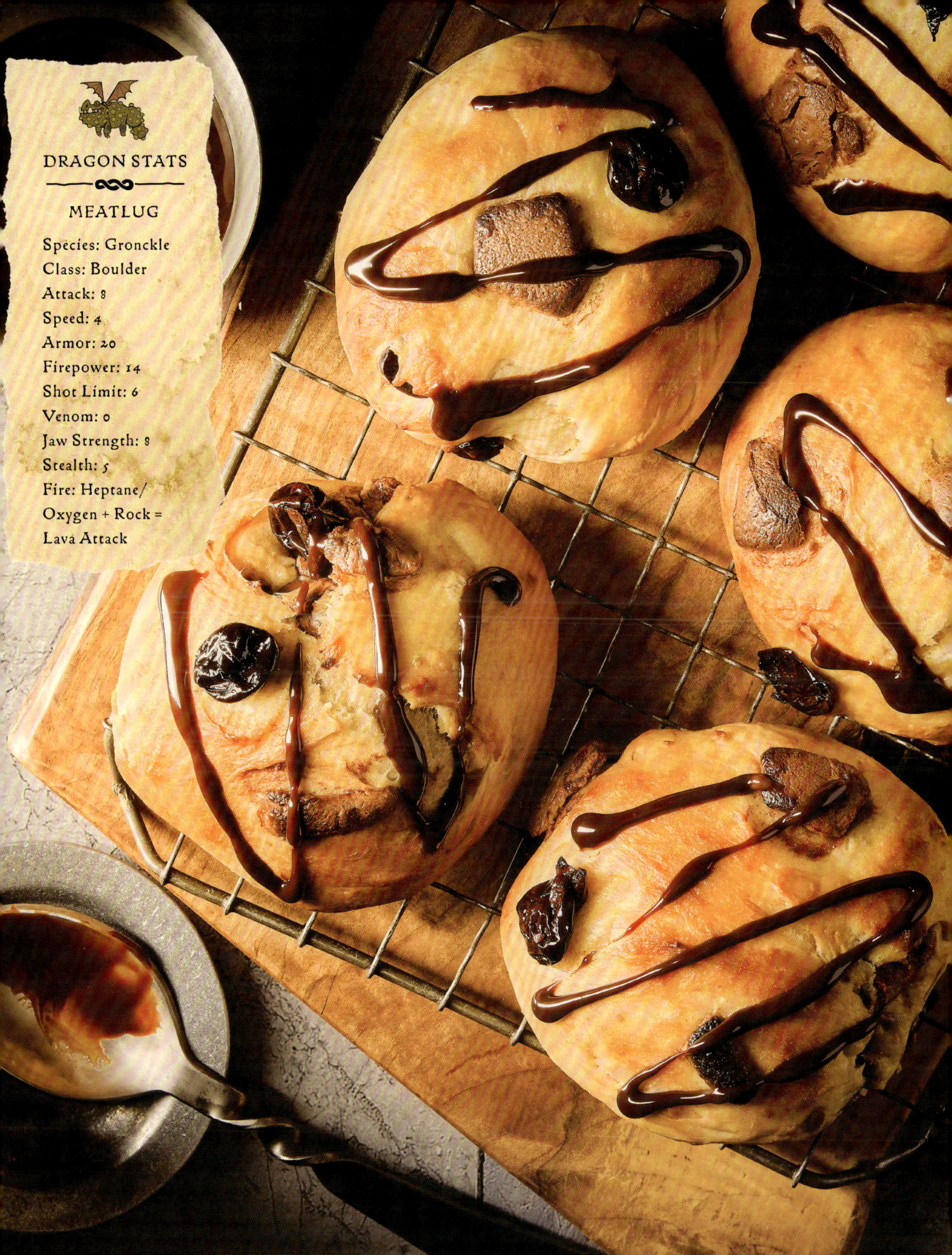
DRAGON STATS
MEATLUG
Species: Gronckle
Class: Boulder
Attack: 8
Speed: 4
Armor: 20
Firepower: 14
Shot Limit: 6
Venom: 0
Jaw Strength: 8
Stealth: 5
Fire: Heptane/
Oxygen + Rock =
Lava Attack

V+*, V, DF* | Makes 2 loaves

TUFFNUT'S BRAIDED BEARD BREAD

Here on Berk, we're proud of a lot of things . . . our history, our seamanship, and our ability to make the best out of the worst. We are, of course, most proud of our dragons, but a close second on the overall list is our luscious Viking hair. (It's not easy to have such great hair when you're always around sea air!) Now, not all Berkians have a full head of hair—but we do all enjoy braiding. If there's no hair to braid, we'll braid our bread dough—and when we do, it always comes out so impressive looking. (I think this bread inspired Tuffnut to create a beard from the braids of his hair, but don't anybody tell him I told you that. He still thinks we don't know that his "full, thick beard" comes from the back of his head, not the front!)

BREAD

1 cup (2 sticks) salted butter (see note)

2 cups whole milk (see note)

1½ teaspoons ground cinnamon

½ teaspoon freshly ground cardamom seeds

2 packets (4½ teaspoons) active dry yeast

⅔ cup granulated sugar, divided

2 eggs, beaten

2 teaspoons Diamond Crystal kosher salt

Up to 6 cups all-purpose flour, divided

2 cups raisins

2 tablespoons melted butter, for greasing and brushing (see note)

HONEY ICING

2 cups confectioners' sugar

¼ cup whole milk (see note)

2 tablespoons honey (see note)

½ teaspoon vanilla extract

SPECIAL TOOLS

Bench scraper

Sifter

TO MAKE THE BREAD: In a small saucepan over medium-high heat, melt the butter, then add the milk and scald—you'll know it's hot enough when it's just shy of boiling and bubbles form around the edge of the pot. Remove from the heat and add the cinnamon and cardamom, letting the spices steep while the milk cools to lukewarm.

Place the yeast and a tablespoon of the sugar in a large mixing bowl, then pour in a half cup of the lukewarm milk, stirring, then letting sit until it bubbles, about 5 minutes.

Stir in the remaining milk and sugar, along with the eggs and salt. Adding a half cup of flour at a time, add 4 cups of the flour and gently mix until the dough begins to pull away from the sides of the bowl. (You may not need the entire amount called for.)

Lightly flour a flat surface and transfer the dough to this, kneading for about 10 minutes. (A bench scraper will help when dough sticks to the surface. See instructions in the tip for Meatlug's Sweet Chocolate and Cherry Buns, page 26.) Add the raisins and scrape the dough into a ball.

Lightly grease a large mixing bowl (feel free to use the same mixing bowl as used to mix the dough, but wipe out any excess dough), then transfer the dough to this, turning it around once so all sides are coated with the oil. Cover with a clean, damp towel and let rise in a warm, draft-free place until doubled, about 1 hour.

Punch the dough down and divide it into two equal portions. To make braided loaves, divide each portion into three equal parts and roll these into three ropes. Press the ends of each together and cross the right log over the center log, then the left log over this, and repeat, as though you're braiding hair. When you reach the end, press these together. Cover with clean, damp tea towels and let rise again until doubled, another hour.

Preheat the oven to 375°F. Brush each loaf with melted butter and bake until golden, about 30 minutes. Let cool on a wire rack.

TO MAKE THE HONEY ICING: Sift confectioners' sugar to remove any clumps and whisk it in a medium bowl with the milk, honey, and vanilla until smooth. Drizzle over the cooled braids and let set before slicing.

*NOTE: To easily make this dairy free and vegan, simply swap out the milk and butter for plant-based alternatives and substitute additional confectioners' sugar for the honey in the icing.

GF, DF | Serves 3

FIRE AND HONEY BACON

It's a well-known fact that most dragons breathe fire. They developed this ability mostly for offense and defense, but with a little training, they can also use it to make some perfectly crisp bacon. It takes some time to teach them the right amount of flame to shoot (unless you like your bacon burnt to a cinder), but once they learn, you'll have perfect bacon every time. You'll just need a little dragon nip and a lot of patience . . . or, if your dragon is feeling stubborn—or is a lava-spitting Gronckle—you can get similar results on your own with 80-proof alcohol and a lighter.

6 thick bacon slices

2 tablespoons honey

3 tablespoons 80-proof alcohol such as whiskey or aquavit

SPECIAL TOOLS

Small measuring cup with a spout

Stick lighter or match

Preheat a large frying pan over medium-high heat and arrange the bacon slices in a single layer. Cook on one side until they begin to brown, then flip each and brush with the honey. Continue cooking until cooked through but not crispy. Turn off the burner and remove the pan from the stove.

Pour the alcohol into a small measuring cup with a spout, then pour this into the pan. Use a stick lighter or match to light the vapors, slightly above the surface of the alcohol. Let burn until the alcohol evaporates and the fire extinguishes.

TIP: Keep a lid on hand in case you need to put the fire out, and always be sure an adult is present when using dragon-inspired cooking methods.

INGERMAN RATING

+8 Crispness
+7 Sweetness
-5 Longevity (it's the first thing gone from my plate!)

V, GF* | Serves 6 to 8

CHIEFTAIN'S CHEESE PIE (FOR STOICK THE VAST)

Hiccup's dad, Stoick the Vast, was one of the best chieftains Berk ever had. He was also one of the biggest and strongest—in fact, I heard he wrestled a dragon once (rumor has it that that was because the dragon was trying to steal his breakfast)! Now, it's true that tamed dragons aren't usually driven to steal most foods. And it's also true that, as a general rule, they're not known to be enamored of cheese . . . but when something smells as good as a cheese pie that's fit for a chieftain as great as Stoick, even dragons can't resist trying to steal a bite!

CRUST

1½ cups all-purpose flour, plus more for dusting (see note)

9 tablespoons cold unsalted butter, cubed

1 tablespoon whole-grain mustard

½ teaspoon Diamond Crystal kosher salt

7 tablespoons ice water, divided

FILLING

2 tablespoons salted butter

6 ounces lacinato kale leaves, roughly chopped

4 eggs

10 ounces aged cheddar, shredded

¾ cup whole milk

½ cup chopped fresh herbs (a mix of chives, dill, and parsley)

SPECIAL TOOLS

Food processor

11-inch tart pan with a removable bottom

Pie weights or dried beans

TO MAKE THE CRUST: Using a food processor, pulse the flour, butter, mustard, and salt until combined and crumbly. Add ice water, starting with about 5 tablespoons and adding more as necessary, pulsing until the dough comes together. Gather it into a disk, wrap it in plastic, and chill in the refrigerator for an hour.

Preheat the oven to 375°F. Remove the dough from the fridge and roll out on a lightly floured surface, forming a circle about a foot in diameter. Carefully lift and set into an 11-inch tart pan with a removable bottom. Cover the dough with a sheet of parchment paper or foil, then fill with pie weights or dried beans (this will weigh down the dough as it bakes). Bake until the crust begins to brown, 15 to 20 minutes. Remove the weights, prick the crust, and keep baking for another 10 to 12 minutes, or until the bottom is golden.

TO MAKE THE FILLING: Melt the butter in a large skillet, then add the kale and sauté over medium-high heat until softened, about 5 minutes. Evenly spoon the sautéed kale over the baked crust.

In a large mixing bowl, beat the eggs, then stir in the cheese, milk, and chopped fresh herbs. Pour over the kale. Bake for about 25 minutes, until the filling is golden and set.

Let cool to room temperature and serve.

*NOTE: To easily make gluten-free, use a one-for-one gluten-free flour blend.

INGERMAN RATING

+10 Savoriness

+8 Viking Cheesiness

+3 Unexpected aromatic appeal to dragons

INGERMAN
RATING
+7 Practicality
+11 Warmth
+25 Potato presence

GF, DF | Serves 6

PYTTIPANNA (LEFTOVER HASH) WITH SWEET POTATO HASH AND FRIED EGGS

Given how hard it can be to grow food here on Berk, it should come as no surprise that Vikings absolutely hate to waste any part of a meal. Unlike dragons, we can't swallow our food in a single gulp (though we can try and have tried) so we look to other ways to make sure nothing goes to waste, like making pyttipanna. I think, pound for pound, pyttipanna is the best way to make use of leftover meats and potatoes. Just combine them with some Sweet Potato Hash (page 68) and Horseradish Crème (page 52) and you can start the day with last night's supper! It's so delicious, you might be tempted to eat the whole batch in one gulp (but I don't recommend it). Good luck . . .

2 tablespoons salted butter

1 pound leftover cooked meat (such as sausages, steak, or chicken), cut into 1-inch pieces (see note)

1 recipe Sweet Potato Hash (page 68)

Diamond Crystal kosher salt

Freshly ground black pepper

Worcestershire sauce, for seasoning

6 fried eggs, for serving

Pickled beets, for serving

Whole grain mustard, for serving

Horseradish Crème (page 52), for serving

In a large frying pan, melt the butter over medium heat. Add the meat and cook until heated through, then add the sweet potato hash and heat another minute or two, stirring once or twice to combine. Season with salt, pepper, and Worcestershire sauce to taste.

Divide into six portions and top each with a fried egg, pickled beets, a dollop of whole grain mustard, and a drizzle of horseradish crème.

CHAPTER TWO | STEWS AND SALADS

A NOTE FROM THE CHIEF ON STEWS AND SALADS

You can be a lot of things in life, but the most important thing to be is adaptable. To be able to adjust or pivot depending on your circumstances. If Berkians weren't capable of that, we'd never have been able to make peace with dragons after 300 years of fighting them!

You know what else is adaptable in Berk? Cauldrons. They have a million uses. Like storage, for starters; I keep most of my spare tools in one. In a pinch, they can also make a pretty good helmet. But their best uses are culinary. (If you're reading this, Tuffnut, culinary means it has to do with food.)

Every good stew—from Gobber's Homemade Yak Noodle Soup (page 42) to Snotlout's Burned Snout Soup (page 40)—starts off in a cauldron. And if you're not into broth, you can use also your cauldron to toss a pretty good salad. Some even come with potatoes now. What'll they think of next?

—Hiccup Horrendous Haddock III

GF | Serves 4 to 6

BERKIAN CREAMY COD AND POTATO STEW

Berk doesn't really have the most hospitable climate for farming crops—but having dragons around to keep the frost at bay for a little while longer with their fiery breath has really helped us make better use of the seeds our trading parties bring back. Well, some of them. Tomatoes still fall apart at even the tiniest hint of frost. And the kohlrabi . . . I don't think we've ever actually grown kohlrabi. But we've done well with anything classified as a root vegetable. Potatoes, one of my favorite root vegetables (they're right up there with carrots, turnips, and parsnips) taste especially good in creamy cod stews; much better than the pine cones we used to use. Now, the key to making this stew is a good, long simmer; that means you bring it to a boil and then back the heat down. Not all dragons have precise enough control of their flame to do this, but a Dramillion does! They can copy any kind of dragon flame, from the highest to the lowest temperature!

- 3 tablespoons salted butter
- 1 white onion, chopped
- 4 cups fish stock
- 1 pound (3 medium) waxy potatoes such as Yukon Gold, peeled and diced
- 2 carrots, peeled and diced
- 1 medium parsnip (5 ounces), peeled and diced
- 1½ pounds cod, cut into 1½-inch pieces
- 1 cup heavy whipping cream
- 2 tablespoons white wine vinegar
- ½ tablespoon granulated sugar
- Generous pinch Diamond Crystal kosher salt
- White pepper
- Curly leaf parsley, chopped, for garnish

In a large pot, melt the butter over medium-high heat. Add the onion and sauté until golden, about 4 minutes. Add the fish stock, potatoes, carrots, and parsnip and simmer for about 12 minutes, until the vegetables soften but are not yet fork-tender.

Add the cod and gently simmer until cooked through, about 8 minutes. Stir in the heavy cream. Add vinegar and sugar and season with salt and white pepper to taste.

Pour in bowls and garnish with a sprinkling of parsley.

DRAGON STATS

Species: Hobgobbler
Class: Mystery
Attack: 8
Speed: 8
Armor: 4
Firepower: 6
Shot Limit: 28
Venom: 0
Jaw Strength: 12
Stealth: 18
Fire: Incendiary Slobber

V*, GF*, DF | Serves 6

HOBGOBBLER'S FAVORITE YELLOW PEA AND HAM STEW WITH HOMEMADE CROUTONS

Not long ago, the Hobgobbler was thought of as a bad omen. Vikings freaked out whenever they saw one. Though they don't normally have an aggressive personality, they do get hungrier than you'd think for something so small . . . and when they get hungry, they go absolutely berserk until they're full again. Can you blame them? No one likes being hungry! Hobgobblers can and will eat anything—from longships to houses—but they also seem to love a good, savory stew stocked with bacon, ham, and vegetables, like this one. I've actually seen them dive into the pot and eat the whole works at once! Once they finish a cauldron or two, they'll go back to being the sweet, curious, adorable little dragons that they are. As with all soups, the dragon-assisted cooking method is all about simmering; just don't let a Hobgobbler try to help! They'll be so excited by the idea of stew, they might just melt your cookpot!

SOUP

2 slices bacon, diced (see note)

1 white onion, chopped

2 cups yellow split peas, rinsed and drained

6 cups chicken broth (see note)

2 medium (about ¾ pound) waxy potatoes such as Yukon Gold, peeled and diced

1 turnip, peeled and diced

3 carrots, peeled and diced

1 rosemary sprig

1 bay leaf

3 cups chopped kale leaves

½ pound ham, cut into ⅓-inch cubes (see note)

Diamond Crystal kosher salt

Freshly ground black pepper

CROUTONS

¼ cup olive oil

4 cups cubed rustic bread (see note)

Fresh thyme leaves

Diamond Crystal kosher salt

TO MAKE THE SOUP: In a large pot over medium heat, fry the bacon until golden. Add the onion and sauté until translucent. Add the peas and broth and bring to a simmer, adjusting the heat to maintain a simmer, partially covered, for 20 minutes.

Tip in the potatoes, turnip, carrots, rosemary sprig, and bay leaf and cook, stirring occasionally, until the peas are mushy, 45 to 60 minutes.

TO MAKE THE CROUTONS: While the soup simmers, preheat the oven to 350°F and set out a large baking sheet. Scatter the cubed bread on the sheet and drizzle with oil. Sprinkle with fresh thyme leaves and salt and toss with your hands until the bread is coated. Bake for 10 to 12 minutes, or until golden and crispy, tossing midway if needed. Set aside.

To finish the soup, add the kale and ham to the pot and simmer until the kale is wilted and the ham is heated through, about 4 minutes.

Remove and discard the rosemary sprig and bay leaf. Season with salt and pepper to taste. Serve with croutons on top.

*NOTE: This recipe can be easily made gluten-free by substituting a gluten-free alternative for the rustic bread. Make it vegetarian by omitting the bacon and ham and adding 2 tablespoons of olive oil for the fat the bacon would have provided, plus substituting vegetable broth for the chicken broth.

GF*, DF* | Serves 6

SNOTLOUT'S BURNED SNOUT SOUP

There's hot food, and then there's REALLY hot food . . . and really hot food is for sure the best way to describe brennsnut, which, if you didn't already know, means "burnt snout." We call it that because this meat-and-veggie stew is supposed to be served hot enough to, well, burn your snout. This reminds me of a fun fact: The average Monstrous Nightmare, like Snotlout's dragon Hookfang, is known to occasionally set themselves on fire—now, that's what I'd call a burnt snout! I wonder if the bond between rider and dragon is the reason Snotlout likes brennsnut so much now? . . . I'll have to investigate further! (I wonder if he has time to fill out a questionnaire?)

1 cup pearl barley (see note)

2 tablespoons salted butter (see note)

1 yellow onion, diced

1 leek, cut in half lengthwise then thinly sliced

6 cups beef broth

2 medium (about ¾ pound) waxy potatoes such as Yukon Gold, peeled and diced

4 carrots, diced

2 celery stalks, diced

1 small (about 1 pound) celeriac (celery root), peeled and diced (see note)

3 thyme sprigs

1 pound cooked meat such as beef, pork, chicken, or sausage, cut into cubes

½ head of cabbage, sliced

½ cup finely chopped fresh herbs such as dill, parsley, or chives

Diamond Crystal kosher salt

Freshly ground black pepper

Rinse and drain the barley. In a large pot, melt the butter over medium-high heat. Add the onion and leek and sauté until lightly golden, then add the barley and broth and bring to a boil. Reduce the heat to maintain a simmer and cook for 30 minutes.

Add the potatoes, carrots, celery, celeriac, and thyme and continue cooking until the vegetables are tender and the barley cooked through, about 20 minutes.

Add the meat and cabbage and cook until the meat is heated through and the cabbage wilted, about 4 minutes.

Stir in the chopped fresh herbs and season with salt and pepper. Remove the thyme sprigs and serve.

*NOTE: To make gluten-free, substitute brown rice or quinoa for the barley, adjusting cooking times as necessary. This recipe can be easily made dairy-free by substituting a dairy-free alternative for the butter. If celeriac (celery root) is unavailable, you can substitute rutabaga.

DRAGON STATS

HOOKFANG

Species: Monstrous Nightmare
Class: Stoker
Attack: 15
Speed: 16
Armor: 12
Firepower: 15
Shot Limit: 10
Venom: 0
Jaw Strength: 6
Stealth: 9
Fire: Kerosene Gel

MONSTROUS NIGHTMARE ABILITY:

Self-immolation (covers its body with fire)

GF*, DF* | Serves 4

GOBBER'S HOMEMADE YAK NOODLE SOUP

As all Vikings know, winter is the longest season. (If you want to get technical, it's actually several seasons; Berkians list false winter, warm winter, cold winter, really cold winter, oh-Odin-how-did-it-get-even-colder winter, and is-this-spring-no-it's-still-winter winter.) With that much wintertime, there are many days where even the toughest among us likes to get under a blanket or two, have some hot food, and enjoy a little coziness. And there's nothing better for a cozy day than Gobber's Homemade Yak Noodle Soup . . . which is actually made from chicken. Why? Well, we were low on yak one year and swapped it out with chicken and you know what? It worked! But we all still call it yak noodle soup anyway because Vikings can be incredibly stubborn. I should add that this is also the perfect meal whenever you have the sniffles! It may not be a cure, but it feels like it. Now, like most good soups, simmering is the key here . . . so get your Dramillion ready and watch that fire closely!

1 rotisserie chicken

2 tablespoons salted butter (see note)

1 white onion, diced

3 carrots, halved lengthwise and cut diagonally into ½-inch slices

3 stalks celery, halved lengthwise and cut into ¼-inch slices

8 ounces cremini or button mushrooms, cut into ¼-inch slices

4 cups chicken stock or broth

½ pound noodles (shape of your choice, see note)

¼ cup fresh herbs (mix of parsley, dill, and chives), finely chopped

Diamond Crystal kosher salt

Freshly ground black pepper

Remove all the meat from the chicken and discard the carcass. Shred and slice the chicken into 1-inch pieces and set aside.

In a large pot, melt the butter over medium-high heat. Add the onion and sauté until translucent, about 4 minutes. Add the carrots, celery, and mushrooms and continue to sauté for another 2 minutes. Pour the stock or broth into the pot and bring to a simmer. Add the noodles and cook according to the timing on the package directions. Tip the reserved chicken into the pot, stir in the herbs, and season with salt and pepper to taste.

*NOTE: To make dairy-free, use a nondairy butter substitute, and to make gluten-free, use gluten-free noodles.

INGERMAN RATING

+0 Yak

+10 Good-for-what-ails-you

+7 Noodling

V, GF | Serves 4

GOTHI'S CREAMY POTATO SALAD WITH HERBS

One thing that we've learned about dragons, something I mention elsewhere in this chronicle, is that they have a real affinity for herbs, which they're easily able to find with their keen sense of smell. Of course, dragon nip is their favorite (my sweet Meatlug gets hers as a special treat every night before bedtime) but they've helped us find so many others, and I have to say, it's really been a gift to Berk's kitchens. Before the dragons, herbs were in such short supply that Gothi's famous potato salad was just a pot of boiled potatoes—and now look what she can do! Speaking of boiling, that's still at the heart of the recipe . . . a nice hot fire will be needed, and any Stoker Class dragon will be able to provide it; the pot will be boiling in no time!

1½ pounds bite-size red potatoes

¼ cup sour cream

2 tablespoons mayonnaise

3 tablespoons whole-grain mustard

1 tablespoon distilled white vinegar

½ teaspoon Diamond Crystal kosher salt

½ cup finely chopped dill pickles

½ cup chopped fresh herbs (ideally a mix of wild garlic, dill, and chives)

In a medium saucepan, bring generously salted water to a boil. Add the potatoes and simmer until tender, about 15 minutes, then drain.

In the meantime, make the dressing. In a medium mixing bowl, whisk together the sour cream, mayonnaise, mustard, vinegar, and salt. Add the potatoes, pickles, and herbs and stir until the potatoes are coated in the dressing.

Serve at room temperature.

INGERMAN RATING

+4 Creaminess

+2 Softness

+13 Potato power

V, GF | Serves 6

VALKA'S CREAMY CUCUMBER AND FENNEL SALAD WITH SKYR AND DILL

Something that not everyone knows is that a significant amount of a wild wolf's summer diet is made up of blueberries! Nature always surprises me. I didn't expect wolves to like fruit at all, but it's totally true—and the funny thing is, it's the same with dragons; when they can get fruit and vegetables, they love them! (Not as much as they love fish . . . or in Meatlug's case, rocks—but almost.) Hiccup's mom, Valka, makes a cucumber salad that I've seen dragons go wild for. I thought maybe they liked the cool, crisp, and refreshing flavor of cucumber as a counterbalance to the fire that they can breathe . . . but Hiccup suggested that it could be the specific herbs in the salad. We all know dragons do love herbs, but in the case of this salad, I'd say that's kind of a big dill.

2 large cucumbers, peeled and thinly sliced

2 teaspoons Diamond Crystal kosher salt

1 cup skyr

¼ cup mayonnaise

2 tablespoons distilled white vinegar

1 teaspoon granulated sugar

Small handful fresh dill, coarsely chopped

½ small bulb fennel, thinly sliced

Arrange the cucumber slices in a single layer on paper towel–lined baking sheets (or any other food-safe surface), sprinkle with salt, and allow the moisture to drain for about 30 minutes. Gather up the slices in the towels and wring out to remove any additional water.

In a medium bowl, whisk together the skyr, mayonnaise, vinegar, sugar, and dill. Add the cucumber slices and fennel and toss to combine. Taste and add more salt if desired.

INGERMAN RATING

+3 Coolness
+12 Herbs
+7 Reminiscence of summer days

V, GF | Serves 4

STORMFLY SLAW

If you've studied your dragons (and why wouldn't you?) you'd already know that a Deadly Nadder has a whole bunch of sharp spines on its tail that it can hurl with a lot of accuracy. And boy, can they pile up! Whenever Astrid finishes training her dragon, Stormfly, for the day, so many discarded spines have pierced our shields and bounced off the arena's rocks—when we gather them up, they make me hungry for this slaw, which features pointy spears of apples and celeriac mixed with cabbage and a smooth and savory sauce. With all those tasty slivers in a dish, this slaw is just as pretty as a Nadder, but nowhere close to deadly.

1 large celeriac, peeled and julienned

¼ head green cabbage, sliced

½ large tart green apple such as Granny Smith, julienned

1 cup sour cream

¾ cup chopped fresh flat-leaf parsley

6 tablespoons distilled white vinegar

2 tablespoon freshly grated horseradish

1 teaspoon Diamond Crystal kosher salt

In a large bowl, combine the celeriac, cabbage, and apple. In a smaller bowl, whisk together the sour cream, parsley, vinegar, horseradish, and salt. Pour this over the slaw and toss to combine.

DRAGON STATS

STORMFLY

Species: Deadly Nadder
Class: Tracker
Attack: 10
Speed: 8
Armor: 16
Firepower: 18
Shot Limit: 6
Venom: 16
Jaw Strength: 5
Stealth: 10

V+*, V, GF*, DF | Serves 6

NORDIC HARVEST SALAD

You've probably been told that Berk has one of the shortest growing seasons known to mankind. (Actually, I think Hiccup says that to anyone who visits the island for the first time, right before he brags about our dragons.)

Hiccup's not wrong, exactly, about the weather—but to be accurate, Berkian farmers have learned how to make the most out of the time they have with hardy, fast-growing crops that get us set up for the winter. Also, the nearby forests are very well stocked with nuts and berries. When you put it all together, at the end of the season, you get the right ingredients for a harvest salad—one of my favorite pre-winter meals!

GRAINS

1 cup ancient grain or wild rice blend, cooked according to package instructions (see note)

¾ cup dried cranberries

½ cup dried blueberries

2 tablespoons salted butter (see note)

Diamond Crystal kosher salt

Freshly ground black pepper

HARVEST

2 ounces baby kale leaves

2 ounces baby arugula

2 ounces red cabbage, thinly sliced

1 cup blueberries

1 large apple, cored and thinly sliced

6 radishes, thinly sliced

SERVING

½ to 1 cup store-bought raspberry walnut vinaigrette

¼ cup seed-based granola (ideally a pumpkin-seed and flaxseed mix)

TO MAKE THE GRAINS: In a large mixing bowl, combine the cooked ancient grain, while still hot, with the dried cranberries, dried blueberries, and butter and season with salt and pepper to taste. Set aside to cool.

TO MAKE THE HARVEST: In another mixing bowl, combine the kale, arugula, cabbage, blueberries, apple, and radishes. Add the cooled grains and stir.

TO SERVE: Drizzle over enough vinaigrette to moisten the grains and vegetables and toss to combine. Divide among six plates, garnish with the granola mix, and serve with additional dressing on the side.

*NOTE: Check your packaging and make certain that your chosen ancient grains or wild rice blend are gluten-free to ensure this is a gluten-free meal. To make this recipe vegan, substitute a vegan alternative for the butter.

INGERMAN RATING

+5 Foraged material

+6 Versatility

-25 Reminder that first winter is coming

A NOTE FROM THE CHIEF ON SAUCES, APPETIZERS, AND SIDES

We've got a lot of sheep on Berk. I mean, you've seen them. And they can go anywhere! If I had a rock for every time I turned around and almost ran into a sheep, I could build a mountain.

. . . And there'd probably be sheep at the top.

But we love having sheep in Berk. They're quiet (mostly). They're serene. They look so darn pleased with themselves. And we couldn't score a Dragon Race without them!

Besides all that, they provide balance. Balance is important in life. For every high-energy dragon bounding around looking to play, there's peaceful sheep. Just . . . staring at you and chewing cud. It's complementary.

The recipes in this chapter are a lot like sheep—not only can they pop up anywhere, but they also provide some great balance to a meal. Remember, balance is important!

You want a side dish that can go with your breakfast or your dinner? That's here (Sweet Potato Hash, page 68). You want something you can munch on for lunch or sneak in as a midnight snack? That's here, too (Raincutter's Rugbrød and Grubs, page 58).

We've even got sauces that'll make most everything taste better no matter what time you decide to chow down (like the Horseradish Crème, page 52).

—Hiccup Horrendous Haddock III

V, GF | Makes 3 cups

HORSERADISH CRÈME

If there's one thing that I recommend for every cooking hall, it's horseradish. I love that it makes me feel like I can breathe fire without actually being super spicy. That's what Gothi would call magic, I think . . . not that I believe in magic, exactly, but if I did, it would be horseradish. When made into the base of a creamy sauce, horseradish really complements the Spitfyre Steak Bowl (page 81) and is a vital part of Stormfly Slaw (page 47). But the thing no one ever talks about is how good it tastes when mixed with a plate of scrambled eggs. I'm adding that to the lexicon as the definition of savory.

- 2½ cups vegan mayo
- ½ cup prepared horseradish
- ½ ounce fresh garlic, minced or pressed
- ¼ lemon juice
- 1 teaspoon smoked paprika
- 1½ teaspoons espelette (see note)
- Diamond Crystal kosher salt
- Freshly ground black pepper

In a medium mixing bowl, whisk together the mayo, horseradish, garlic, lemon juice, paprika, espelette, and season with salt and pepper to taste. If it's too thick, add a little water—the crème should have the consistency of a creamy salad dressing.

*NOTE: If needed, substitute hot smoked paprika, or a mix of smoked paprika and cayenne pepper, for the espelette.

INGERMAN RATING

+8 Spicy-not-spicy
+12 Aroma
+9 Creaminess

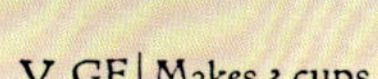

V, GF | Makes 3 cups

HORSERADISH DILL CRÈME FRAÎCHE

With a few extra steps, a few tasty herbs—like parsley and dill—and a little bit of lemon added into the horseradish crème, you totally transform it. In a good way, I mean. This upgraded sauce is kind of like a Dramillion, in a way; it can fit in anywhere. Though the Dramillion fits in by mimicking the flames of other dragons, this condiment fits in by just complementing everything from beef to poultry to pork to seafood to vegetables in a way that nothing else can match. And yes, it's also amazing on scrambled eggs!

2¼ cups sour cream

¾ cup crème fraîche

½ lemon, juiced

6 tablespoons prepared horseradish

¼ cup chopped fresh parsley

2 tablespoons chopped fresh dill

½ teaspoon Diamond Crystal kosher salt

⅛ teaspoon freshly ground black pepper

In a bowl, combine the sour cream, crème fraîche, lemon juice, horseradish, parsley, dill, salt, and pepper and chill until ready to use.

DRAGON STATS

Species: Dramillion
Class: Mystery
Attack: 18
Speed: 14
Armor: 8
Firepower: 20
Shot Limit: 40
Venom: 0
Jaw Strength: 6
Stealth: 8

V, GF*, DF | Makes 3 cups

WILD BERRY BBQ SAUCE

You might think you have the perfect sauce to add to Gobber the Belch's Roasted Turkey Wings (page 84), but unless it's this one, I might have to disagree. (Then again, I'm partial to wild berries—especially blueberries—so I might be slightly biased in this matter.) Anyway, this sauce, with its mixture of berries, adds a little bit of sweet and spicy to any of the meats it meets.

Making this sauce right requires a good simmer in the pot, so don't use too hot a burst of dragon fire! Also, you really need to be careful to not leave this sauce unattended. Though I will warn you, the smell of this berry sauce can drive the sheep of Berk wild, and if you've ever seen a herd of sheep caught up in a berry frenzy, you know they'll turn your house upside down to get a taste! (I don't know if even a dragon could stop them!)

- 1 pound frozen blueberries
- 4 ounces Chambord
- 16 ounces bottled BBQ sauce (see note)
- ½ cup dried cranberries
- ½ cup dried blueberries
- ¼ cup lingonberry jam
- ½ teaspoon Diamond Crystal kosher salt

In a large pot over medium heat, cook the blueberries and Chambord until the alcohol cooks off and the blueberries are thawed. Add the BBQ sauce, dried cranberries, dried blueberries, lingonberry jam, and salt and bring to a simmer. Remove from the heat and let steep 15 minutes. Cool slightly, then blend until smooth. Cool and chill until ready to use.

*NOTE: Ensure your chosen BBQ sauce is gluten-free.

V, GF, DF | Makes ½ cup

CALABRIAN CHIMI

Balance is important. If you have a weapon or a tool that's off-balance, it just doesn't work as well. The replacement tail fin that Hiccup built for his dragon Toothless is another example of how important perfect balance is; if that device wasn't calibrated just right, Toothless wouldn't be able to fly. Balance is also important when it comes to sauces. A good sauce needs to tie different kinds of ingredients together into a satisfying dish . . . and this Calabrian Chimi does that perfectly! It's the right amount of tangy, and it really enhances the potent flavors of the Dragon Fire Chicken Spire (page 82)! I also really like it with the Isle of Gravlax (page 63). (Toothless cocked his head and gave me a strange look the first time he saw me putting the two together, but that's just because he prefers to eat his fish plain.) One more suggestion—try mixing a little bit of this into a bowl of stew . . . it'll blow your mind!

- 1 ounce jarred Calabrian chili peppers in oil
- 8 ounces (½ cup) chimichurri
- ½ teaspoon olive oil
- 1½ tablespoons hot honey
- Pinch Diamond Crystal kosher salt
- Pinch freshly ground black pepper

In a medium bowl, mash the Calabrian peppers in oil with a fork until they have the consistency of a chunky paste. Add the chimichurri, olive oil, and honey and season with salt and pepper to taste. Keep chilled until ready to use.

V+, V, GF, DF | Makes 2⅔ cups

DILL FENNEL CHIMI

The feasts section of this book should make it pretty clear that dill is a really useful herb. It makes seafood sing—I mean, not literally. That would be disturbing. But back to my point—dill is a versatile herb that can also be used in a delicious standalone sauce that pairs very well with fare that doesn't come from the ocean, like crispbreads or roasted vegetables. Of course, going back to ocean-based cuisine, this tangy topping is also the exact thing you want to add to Hiccup's Salmon with Potatoes (page 96). But don't be afraid to experiment! Trying out new combinations of sauces on your favorite dishes can bring about some exciting discoveries! And discovering new tastes is almost as exciting as discovering something new about dragons!

4 ounces white balsamic vinegar

4 lemons, juiced (about 4 ounces)

2 or 3 medium shallots (about 2 ounces), minced

One 3-ounce bunch parsley, finely chopped

One 1-ounce bundle dill, finely chopped

1 large garlic clove, minced

2 teaspoons Diamond Crystal kosher salt

1 teaspoon red pepper flakes

2 cups lemon-infused olive oil

One 1½ pound fennel bulb, minced

In a medium bowl, mix the balsamic vinegar, lemon juice, shallots, parsley, dill, garlic, salt, and red pepper flakes. Gradually pour in the olive oil, whisking constantly, to emulsify. Tip in the minced fennel and stir to combine.

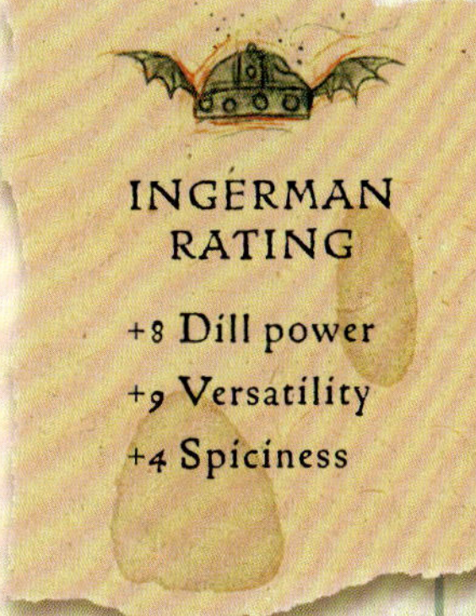

INGERMAN RATING

+8 Dill power

+9 Versatility

+4 Spiciness

V | Serves 4 to 6

RAINCUTTER'S RUGBRØD AND GRUBS

Raincutter dragons are well-known for three things—first, there's their love of inclement weather. Rain is their favorite! Second, there's their sharp claws, which are used to dig through wet soil, which inspired the name of a popular Berkian breakfast treat, Raincutter's Claws (page 134). And of course, there's their favorite snack: grubs. One of the things that you can do to get a dragon's trust while training is to eat with it, but I haven't found many Vikings who love to munch on grubs. It's gross. But the good news is you can trick a Raincutter into thinking you're sharing a meal by substituting rugbrød topped with the much more appetizing buttery sautéed mushrooms! Eat it fast enough and they'll never notice the difference!

12 slices cocktail-size rye bread

2 tablespoons unsalted butter, at room temperature

2 tablespoons cream cheese, at room temperature

¼ teaspoon Diamond Crystal kosher salt

2 tablespoons olive oil

6 ounces oyster and enoki mushrooms

1 teaspoon dried black garlic flakes

Toast the rye bread slices and set aside.

In a small bowl, mash the butter, cream cheese, and salt (to taste) together with a fork until combined. Taste and adjust salt as needed. Set aside.

In a medium skillet, heat the olive oil over medium heat. When it shimmers, tip in the mushrooms and sauté until tender, about 3 minutes. Sprinkle with salt to taste.

To assemble, spread a teaspoon of the butter–cream cheese mixture on each toast and arrange on a platter. Top each with a spoonful of mushrooms, dust with black garlic, and serve.

DRAGON STATS

Species: Raincutter
Class: Sharp
Attack: 8
Speed: 8
Armor: 6
Firepower: 12
Shot Limit: 10
Venom: 6
Jaw Strength: 5
Stealth: 14

GF | Serves 8

HICCUP'S ENDIVE BITES WITH CHEESE AND CURED MEAT

The chief of Berk has a wide range of responsibilities. One of them is keeping up relations with other Viking settlements and their leaders. Something important I've learned from observation is that diplomacy often means feeding people at festivals. You'd think a big feast and an aerial show put on by Dragon Riders and a variety of dragon species would be enough to impress anyone (Meatlug does the best quarter barrel roll), but it's better to overdeliver. Luckily, it doesn't take much to impress even the most resolute Viking clans. Cured meats and light cheese, plus piquant or seasonal berries arranged on a board, and you suddenly have an appetizer worthy of a Gathering of Chieftains.

- 3 endive heads
- 4 ounces prosciutto slices
- 4 ounces goat cheese
- ¼ cup chopped fresh dill
- ½ teaspoon lemon juice
- ¼ cup lingonberry preserves

Cut off the ends of the endive heads and discard them, then arrange the spears on a large platter. Set aside.

Preheat the oven to 350°F and line a baking sheet with parchment. Arrange the prosciutto slices on the parchment and slide the baking sheet into the oven. Bake until lightly crispy, about 8 minutes (watch carefully so they don't overcook). Let cool, then break into bite-size pieces.

In a small bowl, mash the goat cheese, dill, and lemon juice to combine. Spread a little onto each endive spear, then top with ½ teaspoon or so of lingonberry preserves and garnish with prosciutto.

INGERMAN RATING

+10 Impressing neighboring chieftains
+4 Lingonberry presence
+8 Flavor
+6 Variety

GF, DF | Serves 6

ISLE OF GRAVLAX

The Vikings of old had something in common with dragons—well, at least some types of dragons: They would bury fish to preserve them for later. Curing the fish with salt and sugar is a little bit easier all around and, as an added bonus, you're much less likely to find an empty hole in the ground and a happily fed dragon snoozing right next to it when you want to have a nice midnight snack. Gravlax tastes so good with the Calabrian Chimi (page 56), so make sure to whip up a batch of that as well.

- One 1-pound fillet of sushi-grade salmon, skin on, previously frozen
- ¾ cup Diamond Crystal kosher salt
- ¾ cup granulated sugar
- 1 bunch dill, chopped
- 1 tablespoon fresh caraway leaves
- ½ tablespoon freshly ground black pepper
- 1 cup Calabrian Chimi (page 56), for serving

Rinse and dry the salmon. In a shallow dish just large enough to hold the salmon, arrange plastic wrap more than twice the size of the salmon (you'll eventually use it to wrap the fish).

In a small bowl, mix the salt, sugar, dill, caraway, and pepper to combine, then scatter half over the plastic wrap. Set the salmon on this and top with the remaining salt and sugar mix, taking care to cover the entire surface, bottom and top, of the fish. Wrap the plastic around the salmon and slide it into the refrigerator. Chill, turning occasionally, for at least 48 hours.

Unwrap, rinse away the excess curing ingredients, and pat the gravlax dry. Slice thinly and serve with Calabrian chimi.

INGERMAN RATING

+5 Saltiness
+8 Fishiness
+3 Sweetness
+25 Temptation to dragons

V, GF, DF | Serves 4

HONEY- AND LINGONBERRY-ROASTED CARROTS

Root vegetables are a staple on Berk. Anything hearty enough to flourish underground, avoiding the chilly winds that blow as we move from long winter to "Wait, did spring just happen or did a dragon sneeze?" was sort of destined to become beloved. And though potatoes are in the running to be the favorite, naturally sweet carrots make a good case for themselves, too! And when you stoke up a little dragon fire then roast them with honey, look out. Some Vikings use just salt and pepper to season their carrots, but if you add a little more to the mix, as you see below, you'll wind up with something so delicious your favorite dragon might just beg at the table. (I know what you're thinking—but the only root vegetable that makes dragons aggressive is Dragon Root!) Though I could eat these carrots alone—and by the bucketful—they also taste amazing next to Gobber the Belch's Roasted Turkey Wings (page 84) and Hiccup's Salmon with Potatoes (page 96)!

- 1¼ pounds carrots
- 2 tablespoons olive oil
- 2 tablespoons lingonberry preserves
- 1 tablespoon honey
- ½ teaspoon freshly ground cardamom
- 1 teaspoon Diamond Crystal kosher salt
- Fresh thyme, for serving

Preheat the oven to 425°F. Peel and cut the carrots diagonally into ¾-inch slices.

In a medium bowl, combine the olive oil, lingonberry preserves, honey, cardamom, and salt. Add the carrot slices and toss to coat. Tip the carrots onto a baking sheet and roast until tender and slightly caramelized, turning once, about 18 minutes. Transfer to a serving dish and garnish with fresh thyme.

V+, V, GF, DF | Serves 6

ZESTY CIPOLLINI ONIONS

Some feel eating an onion will always be like fighting a dragon used to be—with tears in your eyes. I disagree. I mean, it's perfectly fine if you want your mouth to be on fire and enjoy feeling like you're the next best thing to a Red Death. But it's much better to enjoy your food, in my humble opinion, and onions are one of the tastiest vegetables. This recipe gives you a sweet and mild onion experience and is another side dish that pairs well with just about any savory dish or combination of flavors. Like the Honey- and Lingonberry-Roasted Carrots (page 64), these go so well with Gobber the Belch's Roasted Turkey Wings (page 84) and Hiccup's Salmon with Potatoes (page 96). They just need to be roasted to perfection, which you can manage with any cookfire or a small blast of dragon flame!

2 tablespoons olive oil

1 pound cipollini onions, peeled and trimmed

1 bay leaf

1 tablespoon juniper berries

½ tablespoon peppercorns

Diamond Crystal kosher salt

2 tablespoons apple cider vinegar

Preheat the oven to 350°F.

In a cast-iron (or other oven-safe) pan, heat the olive oil over medium heat, then add the onions, bay leaf, juniper berries, and peppercorns and season with salt to taste. Transfer to the oven and roast, turning occasionally, until golden, about 15 minutes. Remove the pan from the oven and place on a burner over medium heat. Deglaze the pan with apple cider vinegar and continue to cook until deeply caramelized, 2 to 3 minutes.

V+, V, GF, DF | Serves 4

BALSAMIC MUSHROOMS

There are mushrooms all over Berk, and as we all know, not all mushrooms are safe to eat. The good news is that a Snifflehunch's sense of smell is so keen, it can easily sniff out the safe mushrooms from the toxic ones! The bad news is that they can sometimes get distracted with all the other scents in the area. It happens! Luckily, Eret is an accomplished tracker, and he's just as good at hunting mushrooms as he was hunting dragons. Now we have more than we could have ever hoped for, and Gothi's method of preparation here is the best way to eat them—even better than frying them in yak butter! The secret is to roast them just long enough under an even flame and then to mix them into the Spitfyre Steak Bowl (page 81), or alongside Gobber the Belch's Roast Chicken with Beets and BBQ Sauce (page 76). Of course, if you love mushrooms as much as Meatlug and I do, you can eat them right out of the oven!

8 ounces shiitake mushrooms, washed, trimmed, and sliced

8 ounces cremini mushrooms, washed, trimmed, and quartered

⅓ cup olive oil

¼ medium onion, diced (about 2.5 ounces or ¼ cup)

½ teaspoon red pepper flakes

5 tablespoons balsamic glaze

1 garlic clove, minced

1 thyme sprig

1 bay leaf

Scant ¼ teaspoon Diamond Crystal kosher salt

Scant ¼ teaspoon freshly ground black pepper

1 tablespoon chopped fresh parsley

Preheat the oven to 300°F and line a rimmed baking sheet with foil. In a large bowl, mix the mushrooms with the olive oil, onion, red pepper flakes, balsamic glaze, garlic, thyme, bay leaf, salt, and pepper. Tip onto the baking sheet and roast for 20 to 30 minutes, until golden. Remove from the oven, transfer to a serving dish, and scatter with parsley.

V+*, V, GF | Serves 4 to 6

SWEET POTATO HASH

You'd think with so many sizable dragons flying and scurrying around Berk, there would never be any leftovers, even after a feast. But when we manage to save some savory morsels, we mix them into a Sweet Potato Hash, which can be modified to be an accompaniment to a larger meal, or a meal on its own, to say nothing of the fact that it can work for the morning or evening meal. It's a real must for Pyttipanna with Sweet Potato Hash and Fried Eggs (page 33)! And remember, the secret to the perfect hash is to roast the potatoes for just the right amount of time, and under the perfect temperature . . . so don't let your dragon get too excited!

HASH

4 medium (1½ pounds) sweet potatoes, peeled and cut into ¾-inch dice

½ small (2 ounces) white onion, chopped

1 ounce canola oil

½ teaspoon ground cumin

½ teaspoon Diamond Crystal kosher salt

½ teaspoon freshly ground black pepper

FOR SERVING

¼ cup sliced almonds

¼ cup dried cranberries

¼ cup chopped fresh herbs (ideally a mix of dill, parsley, and chives)

2 ounces (½ small log) crumbled goat cheese (see note)

TO MAKE THE HASH: Preheat the oven to 350°F. In a large bowl, toss the sweet potatoes, white onion, oil, cumin, salt, and pepper until the potatoes and onions are evenly coated. Spread this mixture over a large baking sheet and roast, stirring once or twice, for about 25 minutes or until cooked through and crispy. Remove from the oven and cool slightly.

TO SERVE: Top with almonds, cranberries, fresh herbs, and goat cheese.

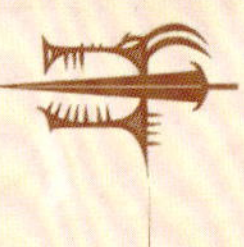

*NOTE: To make a vegan version of this dish, replace the goat cheese with a plant-based alternative.

V, GF | Serves 4

POTATOES WITH CHARRED HERBS

Do you know what a grilled salmon from Hiccup's kitchen has in common with a freshly roasted turkey leg from Gobber's fire pit? I'll give you three guesses—and no, the answer isn't that they're both something a hungry dragon will snatch up when no one's looking!

Actually, I stand corrected. That's also a plausible answer. But the reply I was looking for was this: you'll find roasted potatoes with charred herbs on the dinner plate right next to both Gobber the Belch's Roasted Turkey Wings (page 84) and Hiccup's Salmon with Potatoes (page 96) because it complements both perfectly. To make scrumptious potatoes, the best method is roasting over an ember. I have Meatlug shoot a bit of lava and when it cools a bit, it's the perfect temperature to bury potatoes next to. (You can also use embers from a standard cookfire.)

- Four 6-ounce Yukon gold potatoes
- 2 tablespoons extra-virgin olive oil
- ¼ teaspoon Diamond Crystal kosher salt
- ⅛ teaspoon freshly ground black pepper
- Small bundle of rosemary, sage, and thyme sprigs
- 4 tablespoons (½ stick) salted butter, at room temperature
- 2 garlic cloves, finely minced

Preheat the oven to 350°F and line a small baking sheet with foil. Score each potato with an X, cutting about a quarter of the way down. Toss the potatoes in the oil, salt, and pepper and lay on a sheet pan, cut sides down. Fold up the foil, crimping the ends and enveloping the potatoes inside. Cook until tender, about 40 minutes.

Meanwhile, lightly char the rosemary, sage, and thyme leaves with a brûlée torch or match. Pull off about a tablespoon's worth of herbs and finely chop. Arrange the remaining sprigs on a small platter.

In a small bowl, mash the butter, garlic, and chopped herbs to combine.

Open the foil packet, taking care to avoid steam, and cut each potato open at the X. Nestle each potato among the charred herbs, open side up, then divide the garlic herb butter evenly between the potatoes and serve.

EMBER ROASTING

Prepare a fire outdoors and wrap the potatoes in foil as indicated in the original instructions. Bury the packets in the embers and cook until tender, about 45 minutes.

DRAGON STATS

Species: Gronckle
Class: Boulder
Attack: 8
Speed: 4
Armor: 20
Firepower: 14
Shot Limit: 6
Venom: 0
Jaw Strength: 8
Stealth: 5

V, DF | Serves 6

GOTHI'S CABBAGE AND BARLEY WITH HONEY- AND LINGONBERRY-GLAZED VEGETABLES AND HERBS

Dragons, on their own, are amazing! But when they work together under the direction of their riders—or an alpha—they're even more surprising. And that's what this side dish is like—it combines a warm cabbage-and-barley concoction with Zesty Cipollini Onions (page 65) and Honey- and Lingonberry-Roasted Carrots (page 64) to create something that's more than just a complement to a meal, it's almost a meal in and of itself! Now, even though this dish isn't a stew, we'll still need a little dragon fire to boil some water, because that's how you get your barley ready. Also, be sure to have some Dill Fennel Chimi (page 57) handy, because you definitely need that, too!

1 cup pearl barley

⅓ cup Dill Fennel Chimi (page 57)

½ large head red cabbage, cut into ½-inch-thick slices

1 recipe Honey- and Lingonberry-Roasted Carrots (page 64)

1 recipe Zesty Cipollini Onions (page 65)

¼ cup lingonberry preserves, for serving

Rinse and drain the barley. In a medium pot, bring 3 cups of water to a boil. Add the barley and simmer for about 30 minutes or until tender. Drain and transfer to a large mixing bowl. Stir the chimi into the barley, then add the sliced cabbage, carrots, and onions, tossing briefly to combine. Serve warm with a dollop of lingonberry preserves.

A NOTE FROM THE CHIEF ON FEASTING

Legend says: "If you're going to have a feast at all, then you'd better feast well." At first glance, it's not the most *aspirational* quote, I admit, but it's true. It just took me a little while to figure out why. At first, it felt like it meant that you need to go big or go home. Big food, big mood, right?

But then I realized what it really means. Food is a thing we all need to survive. But a shared meal? That's different. A meal is about more than sharing food. It's about sharing goodwill and good laughs, too. Those good feelings are what bring people (and dragons!) together, and what really makes a bond stick.

In this chapter, Fishlegs collected some of the favorite centerpiece dishes us Berkians turn to for a proper feast. We got a little surf (like Hiccup's Creamy Dill-Poached Haddock with New Potatoes, page 91), a little turf (the Spitfyre Steak Bowl, page 81), and . . . uh . . . whatever word for poultry you can think of that ends in "urf" (Gobber the Belch's Roast Chicken with Beets and BBQ Sauce, page 76). Over these next few pages, you'll find something tasty for the center of any table in Berk. Just make sure your dragons don't snap it up before you can!

—Hiccup Horrendous Haddock III

GF, DF | Serves 4

GOBBER THE BELCH'S ROAST CHICKEN WITH BEETS AND BBQ SAUCE

Berk's resident blacksmith, Gobber, loves roast chicken. I think he loves it more than some Vikings love sailing (although I can't prove that until I come up with a new system of measurement). In any case, roasting chickens is a very high-heat activity, which you would think makes it a perfect job for a dragon like Grump, Gobber's Hotburple. But you'd be wrong—Hotburples spit lava, not fire . . . and even though that's perfect for keeping a forge up and running, it's totally ineffective for cooking, unless you like eating food that's been burnt to a crisp. Luckily for Gobber, the best recipe for roast chicken can also be made with a simple iron pan.

- 1 whole chicken, spatchcocked (see tip)
- 3 tablespoons Diamond Crystal kosher salt
- 1 tablespoon black pepper
- 1 teaspoon dried thyme
- ½ teaspoon dried rosemary
- ¼ teaspoon paprika
- 1 tablespoon olive oil
- 3 large beets, trimmed
- 1 cup Wild Berry BBQ Sauce (page 54)
- 1 recipe Balsamic Mushrooms (page 67) (optional)

SPECIAL TOOLS

- 1 to 2 cups cherry or applewood chips
- Small disposable roasting pan

Twenty-four hours before you want to cook, spatchcock the chicken. In a small bowl, mix together the salt, pepper, thyme, rosemary, and paprika. Coat all the surfaces with this dry rub. Chill in the refrigerator, ideally uncovered.

TIP: Spatchcocking a chicken allows for quicker, more even cooking. Set the chicken breast side down on a cutting board and use kitchen shears to remove the backbone. Flip the chicken over and press down on the breastbone to make it lay flat.

The day of: Place the wood chips in the disposable roasting pan and cover with water. Soak for 1 hour, then drain. Place the pan of chips on the bottom rack of the oven. Preheat the oven to 250°F. Place the chicken in a large cast-iron pan or Dutch oven and brush the top with the olive oil. Nestle the beets in the pan. Cook until it reaches an internal temperature of 140°F, removing the beets early if they're already tender when pierced through with a knife, then increase the oven temperature to 400°F and cook until the chicken reaches 165°F. Rub the skin from the beet, discard, and cut the beets into wedges.

Carve the chicken and serve with the beets, BBQ sauce, and the mushrooms (if using).

DRAGON STATS

GRUMP

Species: Hotburple
Class: Boulder
Attack: 8
Speed: 4
Armor: 20
Firepower: 14
Shot Limit: 6
Venom: 0
Jaw Strength: 8
Stealth 5

V+*, V*, GF, DF* | Serves 4

ASTRID'S SAUSAGE OVER SOUR CABBAGE (SURKÅL) WITH MUSTARD

As recorded, cabbage is one of the crops that grows well on Berk, so we grow and use a lot of it. Surkål is one of the best ways to prepare cabbage; it's a little sour, a little vinegary, and as good as it tastes, it's even better with a hearty sausage. It's a tasty combination that makes a filling meal—but it wasn't always something you could take on the go, until my friend Astrid came up with a trick! If you tuck the sausage and cabbage into lefse, you have a filling, portable snack you can eat while riding your dragon around Berk and beyond! It's so convenient—so grab a few of these and go explore!

4 tablespoons (½ stick) salted butter (see note)

1 medium green cabbage (around 24 ounces), thinly sliced

1 cup white wine vinegar

1 cup vegetable broth

½ tablespoon caraway seeds

1 teaspoon Diamond Crystal kosher salt

4 precooked chicken sausages (One 12-ounce pack) (see note)

Boiled new potatoes, for serving

Stone-ground mustard, for serving

Chopped fresh parsley, for garnish

In a large, heavy pot, melt the butter, then add the cabbage, vinegar, broth, caraway, and salt. Cook over medium-low heat for about 45 minutes, stirring occasionally, until the cabbage is soft and the liquid is reduced.

Meanwhile, heat the sausage according to package instructions. Serve with boiled new potatoes and stone-ground mustard on the side and garnish with parsley.

*NOTE: To easily make this vegan and dairy-free, substitute a plant-based butter alternative and a plant-based sausage for the butter and chicken sausage. Check for "gluten-free" on the sausage packaging if necessary.

GF | Serves 4

SPITFYRE STEAK BOWL

Tough meat is no fun. Vikings don't like it. Even dragons don't like it! Not even the ones who can eat rocks, surprisingly enough! Luckily, we have ways to tenderize meat and make it perfectly delectable. Dragons have caustic saliva that helps soften any tough meat they find. Vikings? Well, because dragon spit isn't very appetizing, we use a savory marinade instead. Marinades make a steak so tender and juicy and full of flavor, you'll even want to use it on cuts of meat that aren't so tough! I even marinate stones for Meatlug from time to time—it doesn't soften them, but she loves a little garlic with her granite! Don't forget to prepare your Balsamic Mushrooms (page 67), Sweet Potato Hash (page 68), and Horseradish Crème (page 52) ahead of time, because you'll want them ready when your steak is done. Together, they make the most amazing meal!

STEAK

1½ pounds flank steak or skirt steak

¾ cup canola oil

Cloves from 1 medium-size garlic bulb, peeled and minced (about 2 ounces)

2 tablespoons Diamond Crystal kosher salt

2 tablespoons freshly ground black pepper

¾ teaspoon seasoned salt

Black truffle spice, to finish

BOWL

2½ cups cooked white rice

1 recipe Balsamic Mushrooms (page 67)

1 recipe Sweet Potato Hash (just the hash part) (page 68)

¼ cup shredded Manchego cheese (1 ounce)

Horseradish Crème (page 52), for serving

TO MAKE THE STEAK: In a shallow dish just large enough to hold the steak (alternatively, use a zip-locking plastic bag), combine the steak, oil, garlic, kosher salt, pepper, and seasoned salt, ensuring the steak is covered by the other ingredients. Marinate for 4 to 6 hours, then grill to the desired temperature, cut into strips, and sprinkle with black truffle spice.

TO PREPARE THE BOWL: Divide the rice among four shallow bowls, then add the mushrooms and sweet potato hash to each serving. Sprinkle with cheese, arrange the steak slices on top, then finish with dollops of horseradish crème.

Serves 4

DRAGON FIRE CHICKEN SPIRE

During my research, I've found that Viking fare used to be very bland. But since the dragons have started helping us find herbs and spices to enhance our food, we've really branched out. Some of us like our food as spicy as dragon fire now—with things like Horseradish Dill Crème Fraîche (page 53), hot honey, and a ton of sauces. This chicken spire has all those flavors and more, and it will have you feeling like you can breathe fire on your own (in the best possible way, of course)! All this talk of heat makes me think of the notorious Red Death . . . a dragon that loved heat so much it nested in a lava-filled volcano! It's a good thing it was immune to being scorched, or it would've been boiled . . . which is exactly how the chicken for the Dragon Fire Chicken Spire needs to be cooked. Wasn't that a great segue? I told Hiccup I was a natural writer . . .

CONES

2 large tortillas, halved

1 teaspoon olive oil

NASHVILLE PULLED CHICKEN

1 pound boneless, skinless chicken breasts or thighs

Diamond Crystal kosher salt

½ cup Nashville-style hot sauce

½ cup hickory BBQ sauce

¼ cup apple cider vinegar

2 tablespoons salted butter

Freshly ground black pepper

GARLIC MAC AND CHEESE

16 ounces elbow macaroni pasta

8 ounces Velveeta cheese sauce

6 tablespoons whole milk

2 tablespoons shredded cheddar cheese

2 teaspoons granulated garlic

SERVING

Calabrian Chimi (page 56), for serving

Fried onions, for serving

TO MAKE THE CONES: Preheat the oven to 375°F. On a parchment-lined baking sheet, arrange each tortilla half and brush with oil. Roll into a cone shape and secure with a toothpick. Bake until crispy, about 5 minutes. Wrap in parchment paper and secure with a piece of tape. Set aside.

TO MAKE THE CHICKEN: In a large pot, arrange the chicken and cover with an inch or so of water. Season with salt. Bring water to boil, simmer until cooked through and reaches 165°F, about 15 minutes. Remove from the water and shred with a mixer or two forks. Set aside.

Drain the pot and add the hot sauce, BBQ sauce, vinegar, and butter and bring to a simmer, stirring occasionally. Add the chicken and mix. Season with salt and pepper to taste.

TO MAKE THE MAC AND CHEESE: In a large pot, bring salted water to a boil. Add the pasta and cook for 10 minutes, or until tender, then drain and set aside.

In the same (now empty) pot, combine the cheese sauce and milk and stir over medium heat until melted. Add the shredded cheddar and granulated garlic and stir until melted. Tip the cooked pasta into the sauce and mix to coat. Set aside and keep warm.

TO SERVE: Arrange each parchment-wrapped cone in a wide glass (such as double old-fashioneds) to keep upright. Add a cup of mac and cheese, followed by ¼ cup of pulled chicken. Top with Calabrian chimi and fried onion and serve.

DRAGON STATS

Species: Red Death
Class: Stoker
Attack: 28
Speed: 7
Armor: 30
Firepower: 27
Shot Limit: 9
Venom: 0
Jaw Strength: 22
Stealth: 2

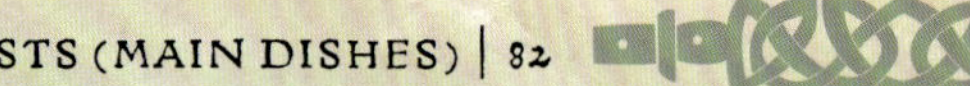

GF* | Serves 4

GOBBER THE BELCH'S ROASTED TURKEY WINGS

In the short time since I completed my first round of notes for this chapter—where I mentioned how much Gobber loved roasted chicken—he's already discovered a new favorite: turkey. Turkeys are like a class 8 chicken—they're bigger, more stubborn, and have a bit of a mean streak. (Does that mean, in this case, Gobber is what he eats?) As the heading suggests, roasting is the best method of preparing turkey, with the same slow, even heat you would use to roast a chicken. But turkey benefits from a sauce with just a little bit more wild berry sweetness, like Wild Berry BBQ Sauce (page 54).

4 pounds turkey wings (about 4 wings)

Olive oil, for drizzling

Diamond Crystal kosher salt

Freshly ground black pepper

1¼ cups Wild Berry BBQ Sauce (page 54) (see note)

1 recipe Potatoes with Charred Herbs (page 71)

1 recipe Honey- and Lingonberry-Roasted Carrots (page 64)

1 recipe Zesty Cipollini Onions (page 65)

¾ cup Horseradish Dill Crème Fraîche (page 53)

Preheat the oven to 425°F. Rinse the turkey wings and pat dry. Place in a medium bowl and drizzle with olive oil and sprinkle with salt and pepper. Turn to coat. Arrange the turkey wings in a roasting pan with a rack. Roast, turning once, until they reach 165°F inside and are crisp on the outside, about 40 minutes. Use a pastry brush to coat with the BBQ sauce.

Serve with potatoes, carrots, onions, and the horseradish dill crème fraîche.

*NOTE: Easily gluten-free if all components contain only gluten-free ingredients (such as the bottled BBQ sauce in the Wild Berry BBQ Sauce).

INGERMAN RATING

+6 Tenderness

+4 Moistness

+1 Size

GF* | Serves 6

STOICK'S RUSTIC BAKED MEATBALLS WITH HONEY GRAVY AND GEITOST

Nobody knows the true origin of the meatball. I've looked through chronicle after chronicle and I still can't figure out who the first Viking to make them was, but everyone in the village has a family story about them. Gobber thinks one reason that they're so popular is because round food would've made for a good projectile back in the old days if—or when—a dragon attacked during a meal. He didn't speculate on what meatballs that could drive dragons away might be made of. He also said meatballs were one of the foods that helped Vikings grow big and strong and pointed out that they were a regular meal of his best friend, Stoick, the biggest and strongest chieftain Berk has ever had. We may never know where meatballs come from . . . but we know how to make them well now!

MEATBALLS

2 tablespoons salted butter

1 medium onion, finely chopped

1 cup rolled or old-fashioned oats (see note)

4 eggs, beaten

½ cup beef broth

2½ teaspoons Diamond Crystal kosher salt

¼ teaspoon ground allspice

¼ teaspoon ground nutmeg

¼ teaspoon freshly ground black pepper

2½ pounds ground meat (beef and pork)

SAUCE

3 tablespoons salted butter

3 tablespoons all-purpose flour (see note)

2¾ cups beef broth

¾ cup heavy cream

½ cup shredded geitost (optional)

¼ cup honey

1 tablespoon fresh thyme leaves

½ teaspoon Diamond Crystal kosher salt, plus more as needed

White pepper

TO MAKE THE MEATBALLS: In a large pan over medium-high heat, melt the butter. Add the onion and sauté until translucent, about 5 minutes.

In a large mixing bowl, combine the sautéed onions, oats, eggs, broth, salt, allspice, nutmeg, and pepper, whisking to combine and break up the eggs. Add the meat and stir or work in with your hands, just until combined.

Preheat the oven to 375°F and line a baking sheet with parchment. Shape the meat into balls about 1½ inches in diameter. Bake in the center of the oven until they reach an internal temperature of 165°F, 15 to 20 minutes.

TO MAKE THE SAUCE: While the meatballs bake, make the sauce. In a saucepan, melt the butter over medium heat. Add the flour and whisk constantly until it thickens, then add the beef broth gradually, allowing it to thicken slightly between each addition. Continue with the cream. When golden and thickened, stir in the geitost (if using) until melted, then stir in the honey, thyme, salt, and pepper. Taste and adjust the salt and pepper if needed.

Transfer the meatballs to a platter, cover with the sauce, and serve.

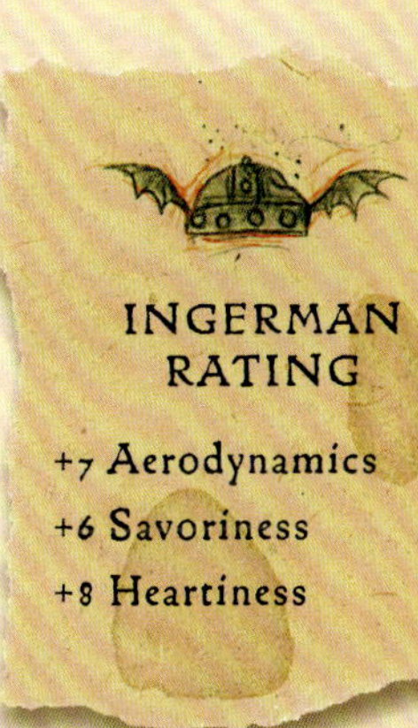

*NOTE: Easily make gluten-free by substituting gluten-free flour for the all-purpose flour and ensuring the oats are gluten-free.

GF, DF* | Serves 8

STOICK'S ROAST PORK WITH VINEGARY RED CABBAGE (RØDKÅL) AND APPLES

When it's time for one of the big feasts of the year—such as Snoggletog, or a name day celebration for an important Berkian chief—roast pork is traditionally the top choice. It was only recently that Chief Stoick decided to add apples and cabbage as accompaniments to the roast going forward. Why apples and cabbage? He was the chief, and he didn't need to explain himself to anyone. (But I'm guessing it's because they taste good with pork.) Like the name suggests, roasting is the only way to cook this dish. A hot, even flame from your favorite dragon works best, but a hot oven, as always, can work in a pinch.

PORK

One 3- to 4-pound pork belly with skin (ribbe)

Diamond Crystal kosher salt

Freshly ground black pepper

CABBAGE AND APPLES

5 tablespoons salted butter (see note)

1 medium red cabbage (around 24 ounces), thinly sliced

2 cups red wine vinegar

½ tablespoon caraway seeds

2 teaspoons Diamond Crystal kosher salt

2 red apples, cored and cut into 8 wedges each

¼ cup lingonberry preserves

Curly parsley, chopped, for garnish

Preheat the oven to 400°F.

TO MAKE THE PORK: Score the skin of the pork belly using a sharp knife, giving it a crosshatch or diamond pattern. (Cut all the way through the fat without cutting the meat itself.) Wipe the skin with a paper towel until dry, then sprinkle with salt and pepper, taking care to work it between the cuts. Place it, skin side up, on a rack in a roasting pan and roast until the internal temperature reads 145°F, about 1½ to 2 hours.

TO MAKE THE CABBAGE AND APPLES: In a large, heavy pot, melt the butter, then add the cabbage, vinegar, caraway, and salt. Cook over medium-low heat for about 45 minutes, stirring occasionally, until the cabbage is soft and the vinegar is reduced and mellowed. Add the apple wedges and cook another 15 minutes or so, until soft. Stir in the lingonberry preserves.

Serve the pork with the cabbage and apples on the side. Garnish with parsley.

*NOTE: To make a dairy-free version of this recipe, use a plant-based butter alternative.

GF | Serves 4

FLAKY PAN-SEARED COD WITH POTATOES, CREAMED GREENS, AND DILL

Living with dragons has made seafood so much easier to come by—trawling with nets worked well, but not as well as Hiccup's latest inventions and our dragon friends skimming the sea to scoop the fish right out of the water! With their air speed, the dragons can collect as many fish in one day as we could in a week with our boats and nets! Truly, they're the wonder of our age. For this pan-seared cod, get a dragon who spits a very hot flame (a Deadly Nadder comes to mind), that will give you a cookfire hot enough to properly sear the fish and boil the water for the potatoes, all at once!

POTATOES

2 pounds russet potatoes, peeled and cut into 2-inch pieces

½ cup (1 stick) salted butter, at room temperature, cubed

¼ cup whole milk

Diamond Crystal kosher salt

FISH

1½ pounds cod fillets, deboned

1 tablespoon olive oil, plus more for greasing

½ teaspoon Diamond Crystal kosher salt

GREENS

2 tablespoons salted butter

1 leek, white and light green parts only, thinly sliced

1 large head cabbage, cut into 1-inch strips, core discarded

1 cup heavy whipping cream

1 cup green peas

¾ teaspoon Diamond Crystal kosher salt

Handful chopped fresh dill

Thinly sliced scallions, for serving

Preheat the oven to 425°F.

TO MAKE THE POTATOES: In a large pot of salted water, boil the potatoes until tender. Drain the potatoes and return to the empty pot. Nestle cubes of butter among the potatoes, mashing the butter into the potatoes as it melts. Add a little milk to achieve a slightly creamy consistency. Taste and season with more salt if necessary.

TO MAKE THE FISH: While the potatoes cook, place the fish on a lightly oiled baking sheet or dish and brush with olive oil and season with salt. Cook the fish until opaque and cooked through, about 15 minutes.

TO MAKE THE GREENS: In a large skillet, melt the butter and cook the leek until it softens, about 5 minutes. Add the cabbage, about ½ cup of water, and bring to a simmer. Cover and continue to cook for 5 to 10 minutes, until the cabbage is tender.

TIP: Remove the lid occasionally and make sure there's enough water, but also that it's evaporating—it should be gone by the end.

Add the cream and peas and bring nearly to a simmer, until tiny bubbles are forming, stirring occasionally over low heat for about 10 minutes until thickened. Stir in the salt and dill and season with more salt, if desired.

To serve, divide the potatoes among the plates and top with the fish. Spoon the creamed greens on the side. Garnish with scallions.

GF | Serves 4

HICCUP'S CREAMY DILL-POACHED HADDOCK WITH NEW POTATOES

It's a well-known fact that Vikings go hand in hand with the ocean. (You can't even be a Viking if you don't live close to open water, which is totally a rule, I read it in the village annals.) Some of us are so connected to the sea that we are even named after fish, and I'm not just talking about me! Chief Hiccup's surname is actually Haddock, which is also the name of a tasty fish—one that's a particular favorite of most Tidal Class dragons, I might add! Given that Hiccup's family is so associated with haddock, you know that he had a recipe lying around—of course, that didn't include any dill or potatoes, so we added those to spice things up. (There's nothing wrong with modernizing.) Now, Hiccup says the family secret is to simmer the fish not in water . . . but rather in milk! Don't let your dragons get the fire too hot—milk doesn't like to be boiled as much as water does!

2 cups whole milk

½ cup heavy whipping cream

1½ pounds haddock fillets, rinsed

4 parsley sprigs

2 dill sprigs, plus 2 tablespoons chopped fresh dill, reserved for serving

3 garlic cloves, quartered

1 bay leaf

½ yellow onion, sliced

1 tablespoon Diamond Crystal kosher salt

Ground white pepper (optional)

¾ pound new potatoes, cooked, for serving

In a skillet or pan just big enough to hold the fish in a single layer, bring the milk and cream nearly to a boil, until tiny bubbles rise to the surface, then reduce the heat to maintain a gentle simmer. Add the fish, parsley, dill, garlic, bay leaf, onion, and salt and cook until the fish is cooked through, about 8 minutes depending on the thickness of the fillets.

Remove the fish from the milk and arrange in shallow bowls with the cooked potatoes. Discard the bay leaf from the poaching liquid. Taste and add salt and pepper if needed. Pour some of the poaching liquid over the fish and scatter with the reserved chopped fresh dill.

GF*, DF* | Serves 4

TERRIBLE TERROR'S DILLED PRAWNS

Terrible Terrors have a class 10 need for engagement. You gotta keep them busy or they'll get into all kinds of trouble! Helping with this recipe is a great way to keep them occupied. You can have them get the fire going to boil a pot of water (their flames are precise) and their tiny-by-comparison-to-most-dragons' claws make short work of getting through the prawns' shells!

2 pounds unpeeled prawns

Salt

1 bunch dill, left whole

1 large lemon, quartered, plus more lemon wedges for serving

2 bay leaves

8 slices white bread (see note)

½ cup (1 stick) best-quality salted butter (see note)

Rinse the prawns and set aside.

In a large pot, bring generously salted water to a boil and add the dill, lemon, and bay leaves. Let simmer for about 10 minutes. Add the prawns and cook for about 3 minutes, depending on the size of the prawns, until pink and opaque.

Spread each slice of bread with butter to eat along with the prawns. Serve with lemon wedges.

*NOTE: Easily make gluten-free and dairy-free by using gluten-free bread and a plant-based butter alternative.

DRAGON STATS

Species: Terrible Terror
Class: Stoker
Attack: 8
Speed: 10
Armor: 6
Firepower: 12
Shot Limit: 10
Venom: 12
Jaw Strength: 2
Stealth: 12

GF* | Serves 4

FISHLEGS'S FISH STICKS WITH NEW POTATOES AND DILL

You know, it would solve a lot of problems if humans could survive on rocks like a Hotburple or a Gronckle can, but don't try it! (I did once. My teeth hurt for a week.) Even the toughest-jawed Vikings are better suited to human fare. I came up with this method myself—I baked breaded strips of cod in an oven, and they're not only easier to chew than a rock, they taste amazing! I tried to name them "fishlegs" after me, but everyone else agreed fish sticks sounded much better. I guess history will be the judge!

FISH

2 pounds cod fillets, cut into 1½-inch-wide sticks

2 teaspoons Diamond Crystal kosher salt

1 cup all-purpose flour (see note)

2 large egg whites

1½ cups panko breadcrumbs (see note)

SAUCE

¾ cup mayonnaise

¼ cup plain Greek yogurt

½ cup finely chopped pickles

2 tablespoons finely chopped fresh dill

2 tablespoons finely chopped fresh parsley

2 teaspoons Dijon mustard

2 teaspoons lemon juice

¼ teaspoon Diamond Crystal kosher salt

FOR SERVING

Boiled new potatoes

Roughly chopped fresh dill

TO MAKE THE FISH: Preheat the oven to 400°F and line a baking sheet with parchment. Rinse and pat dry the fish. Season with salt.

Line up three shallow bowls. In one, place the flour. In the second, whisk the egg whites. In the third goes the panko. Dredge both sides of the fish in the flour, then the egg whites, then the panko.

Arrange the fish in a single layer on the prepared baking sheet. Bake for about 18 minutes, flipping once, until golden and crispy on the outside and the internal temperature reaches 145°F.

MEANWHILE, MAKE THE SAUCE: In a medium bowl, stir together the mayonnaise, Greek yogurt, pickles, dill, parsley, mustard, lemon juice, and salt. Taste and adjust the mustard, lemon juice, and salt to taste.

Serve the fish sticks with the sauce, potatoes, and a scattering of fresh dill.

*NOTE: Easily make this gluten-free by using gluten-free flour and gluten-free panko.

GF | Serves 4

HICCUP'S SALMON WITH POTATOES

Have you noticed how many of these seafood recipes include dill? Well, there are a couple of very good reasons for that. The first is that dill grows really well in a northern climate, so we always have plenty on hand. And second, it tastes so good with fish of all kinds. If I were to pick a favorite dill-based recipe (outside of my innovative Fishlegs's Fish Sticks, that is, which is the best), it would have to be the sauce that Hiccup uses whenever he grills salmon. I still don't know where he got the idea to include fennel . . . Anyway, as the title suggests, the salmon in this recipe needs to be grilled, and if you're going to use a dragon to set the fire, make sure you shoo them away before you start to cook, or they might decide to sneak off with your dinner before it's even finished!

FISH

Four 6-ounce salmon fillets

2 tablespoons extra-virgin olive oil, plus more for greasing

¼ teaspoon pastrami seasoning

½ teaspoon Diamond Crystal kosher salt

FOR SERVING

Dill Fennel Chimi (page 57)

Potatoes with Charred Herbs (page 71)

Honey- and Lingonberry-Roasted Carrots (page 64)

Zesty Cipollini Onions (page 65) (optional)

Horseradish Dill Crème Fraîche (page 53)

TO MAKE THE FISH: Preheat the oven to 400°F. Place the salmon in a lightly oiled baking dish, brush with olive oil, and season with pastrami seasoning and salt. Bake for about 20 minutes, or until the internal temperature reaches 145°F.

Divide the salmon among four plates and spoon dill fennel chimi on top.

TO SERVE: Plate with the potatoes, carrots, and onions (if using) and a generous dollop of Horseradish Dill Crème Fraîche on the side.

GF, DF | Serves 2 to 4

WHOLE SALT-CRUST ROASTED FISH

Dragons love fish. I think it's safe to say that it's their favorite food of all time. They can catch it by the barrelful, and most can swallow whole fish in one gulp! This recipe makes whole fish more palatable for fellow Vikings—you'll want to take your time enjoying every bite. Especially if you like a flaky crust and mushroom stuffing! You'd think a whole fish recipe like this might be made by grilling, but we hit this with dry heat on all sides, which is another way to say we roast it evenly. Be sure your dragons are off exploring or napping while you prep. Otherwise, they will cause chaos trying to get at your main ingredient.

MUSHROOM FILLING

2 tablespoons olive oil

4 ounces cremini mushrooms, sliced or roughly chopped

½ teaspoon Diamond Crystal kosher salt

Leaves from 2 thyme sprigs

1 lemon, sliced

FISH

2 pounds Diamond Crystal kosher salt

¾ cup water

One 1½ pound whole trout or mackerel, cleaned and gutted

1 tablespoon olive oil, for brushing

Preheat the oven to 400°F.

TO MAKE THE MUSHROOM FILLING: In a medium skillet over medium-high heat, heat the olive oil until it shimmers. Add the mushrooms and salt and sauté until softened, about 5 minutes. Stir in the thyme leaves. Set aside, along with the lemon slices.

TO MAKE THE FISH: Line a rimmed baking sheet or dish with parchment paper. In the center of the paper, mix the salt and water, using only enough water to dampen the salt. Scoot two-thirds of it to the side, leaving a thin layer at the bottom on which to place the fish.

Brush both sides of the fish with olive oil, then place the fish on the salt. Stuff the cavity with the mushrooms and lemon slices. Cover the fish with the salt, packing it evenly around. Roast for about 18 minutes, until the fish reaches about 135°F. (The safe internal temperature is 145°F, but it will continue to heat while resting.) Allow the fish to rest for 2 to 3 minutes, then crack open the salt crust with the tip of a sharp knife.

TIP: Start at the bottom and crack it lengthwise.

Discard the salt crust and serve.

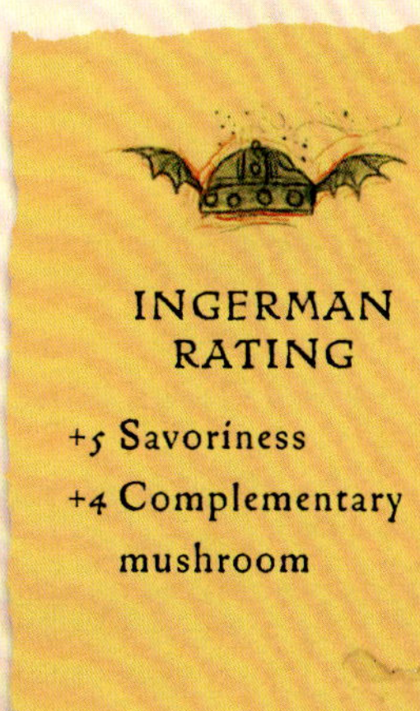

A NOTE FROM THE CHIEF ON GROG

There's this old Viking saying, "You can't have food without drink."

For anyone who remembers what Berkian cuisine used to be, that's not so much advice or observation as it is a desperate warning. Our food used to be so dry it could've parched the sea.

But I think there's more to it. A refreshing drink—from fresh water to Dragon Spit Cider (page 105)—can add a lot to a meal. Cleanse the ol' palate. Cool you down. Warm you up! Refresh you!

Here on Berk, we take pride in what we wet our whistles with, from Snoggletog favorites like Gløgg for Snoggletog (page 111) and Astrid's Yaknog (page 102) to my dad Stoick's Homemade Bubbly Almost-Mead (page 115).

On the next few pages, you'll find all kinds of things that are fit to chug alongside your favorite feast.

—Hiccup Horrendous Haddock III

V, GF | Makes 4 drinks

ASTRID'S YAKNOG

Yaknog has a brief but notable history, and, like many things here on Berk, it kind of started with stubbornness. You see, our beloved Snoggletog holiday has a lot of really, really old traditions, but not a whole lot of recent ones, and sometimes that reads like a challenge. Astrid, a high-caliber Dragon Rider, decided we needed something new (after all, we train dragons now after eons of fighting them), and she picked a new traditional drink, which is where yaknog came from. It's her own recipe. If I'm being honest, and historical records should be honest, her first attempts were, let's just say, less than drinkable. (Poor Meatlug tried a sip from her first batch and flew off with her tail between her legs.) But Astrid is not one to give up. The recipe was refined until it was so good that it became a part of the Snoggletog tradition that we all look forward to!

- One 3.4-ounce package vanilla-flavored instant pudding mix
- 4 cups whole milk
- 2 teaspoons almond extract
- ½ cup granulated sugar
- 2 teaspoons cinnamon
- ½ teaspoon nutmeg
- ⅛ teaspoon salt
- Freshly grated nutmeg, for serving (optional)

In a large bowl, whisk the pudding mix, milk, almond extract, sugar, cinnamon, nutmeg, and salt until the powder is dissolved and the drink is frothy. Taste and adjust the sugar and spices if desired. Serve immediately or chill; keep in mind that the yaknog will thicken with time, so you might want to add more milk to reach your desired consistency.

To serve, divide among four glasses and dust with freshly grated nutmeg, if using.

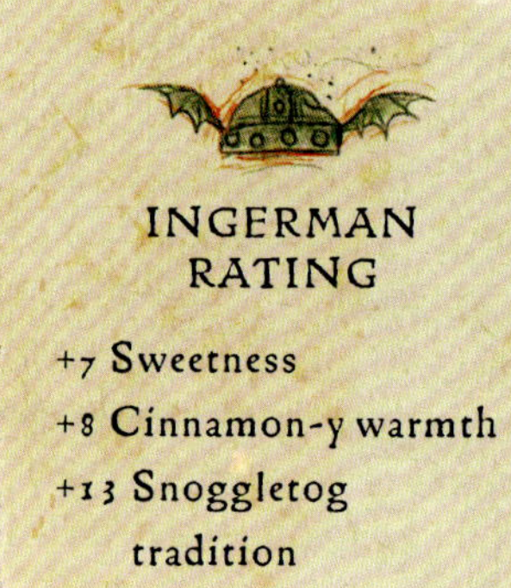

V, V+, GF, DF | Makes 4 drinks

DRAGON SPIT CIDER

When a wild dragon gets annoyed, they attack with a bite or a scratch, or they breathe fire—all of which are just so very painful. But the dragons on Berk are more settled down, and they show annoyance in other ways—most notably, spitting (no one believes me, but I think they learned it from the yaks). Dragon spit isn't as fiery as dragon breath, but it's still very acidic. You really wouldn't want to get any on a parchment cut—but it did give me the idea of spicing up an average spiced cider with an extra kick of tartness. Most people aren't going to want to use dragon spit for that, but lemon juice is a perfect substitute. It really opens up the cider—give it a try!

4 cups apple juice or apple cider

2 cinnamon sticks

6 cardamom pods

One 2-inch strip lemon peel

6 whole cloves

2 tablespoons lemon juice

Sugar, for serving (optional)

In a medium saucepan, combine the apple juice, cinnamon sticks, cardamom pods, lemon peel, and cloves over medium heat. Bring to a simmer, then lower to low heat and simmer for 15 minutes. Strain out the spices. Pour in the lemon juice. Taste and add sugar if desired. Pour in four mugs and serve.

INGERMAN RATING
+3 Leafiness
+7 Coziness
+10 Smokiness

V, V+, GF, DF | Makes 1 cup tea blend, about 16 cups of tea

HICCUP AND TOOTHLESS'S SMOKY STRAWBERRY BLACK TEA BLEND

Though dragon nip will always be the preferred herb of dragons, they also seem to enjoy the smell of good tea brewing. (Did you know tea could be considered an herb? There has been a little debate about this in village meetings, but because herbs are leaves and teas are leaves, I come down on the side of tea being an herb—and Meatlug agrees with me.) This blend is particularly attractive to dragons, because it not only has a strong scent to it, there's also just a little touch of smoke to the taste.

- ½ cup loose-leaf black tea
- ½ cup loose-leaf Lapsang souchong
- ½ cup crushed freeze-dried strawberries
- ½ cup dried culinary-grade rose petals

In a jar, combine the black tea, Lapsang souchong, freeze-dried strawberries, and rose petals, cover, and shake to combine. To serve, add 1 heaping tablespoon to a tea strainer. Pour 1 cup of boiling water over the tea and steep for 4 minutes.

Enjoy black or serve with sugar and cream if desired.

Store unused dried tea blend in an airtight container. This should keep for several months.

V, GF | Makes 2 drinks

BEWILDERBEAST'S ICY SKYR

The Tidal Class Bewilderbeast is one of the most powerful—if not the most powerful—species of dragon that's ever been seen . . . and we've only ever seen two! (There was the first Alpha, a gentle giant that allowed Hiccup's mom, Valka, to live with the dragons under its care for many years . . . and then there was the even larger and less-gentle giant that Drago Bludvist raised from a hatchling, it was all about war!) Both Bewilderbeasts I've seen were enormous; the biggest dragon you can imagine. Second, both were able to compel all other dragons to follow their orders. But the most interesting thing about Bewilderbeasts to me, as a keeper of dragon lore, is the fact that they are the rare breed that emits icy blasts instead of fire. From the thinnest layer of frost to the biggest boulder of ice, their breath runs cold, like this chilled drink we've named in this rare dragon's honor.

One 5-ounce container vanilla skyr

1 cup ice cubes

½ teaspoon iridescent edible glitter powder

1 cup clear cream soda

In a blender, combine the skyr and ice cubes until the ice is crushed and the skyr frothy. Divide between two tall glasses. Add edible glitter powder to each glass. Top with soda and stir to swirl the glitter throughout.

INGERMAN RATING

+6 Sweetness

+2 Brain freeze possibility

+10 Coolness

DRAGON STATS

VALKA'S BEWILDERBEAST

Species: Bewilderbeast

Class: Tidal

Attack: 50

Speed (Land): 6

Speed (Underwater): 18

Armor: 38

Firepower: 60

Shot Limit: 8

Venom: 0

Jaw Strength: 48

Stealth: 2

Fire: Has icy breath that freezes water.

INGERMAN
RATING
+10 For use of ø
+7 Smoothness
+20 Tradition

V, V+, GF, DF | Makes 4 drinks

GLØGG FOR SNOGGLETOG

On Berk, we have a long winter—so long, it can be measured in inches. (Not inches of snow—we don't like to count that high—but in inches of beard hair grown. Winter lasts about six and a half inches.) With such long winters, it's nice to have something heartwarming (and body warming!) to look forward to—and what we look forward to most is the Snoggletog holiday, a traditional time for family and friends and dragons to come together and feast and sing. And then feast some more. (Snoggletog is roughly 5/8 feasting.) Gløgg is the oldest part of the traditional meal—no Snoggletogg feast is complete without it.

12 ounces tart cherry juice
12 ounces cranberry juice
¼ cup raisins
1 cinnamon stick
4 cardamom pods
4 whole cloves
One 2-inch strip orange peel
Granulated sugar, for serving (optional)

In a medium pot, heat the cherry juice, cranberry juice, raisins, cinnamon stick, cardamom pods, cloves, and orange peel over medium-high heat. Bring it almost to a boil, then lower the heat and simmer, covered, for about 30 minutes. Taste and add sugar, if needed, to reach the sweetness you desire. Ladle into four mugs, adding a few raisins to each and discarding the rest of the solids.

V, V+, GF, DF | Makes 2 drinks

BARF AND BELCH'S SWEET-AND-SOUR SEA BUCKTHORN SMOOTHIE

It's been pretty well established that the Zippleback's two heads can lead to a lot of contradiction. Sometimes, it's hard to get a Zippleback's two minds on the same page . . . but other times, their differences complement each other, and you get something totally unique and amazing—like their flaming wheel of death! That's the idea behind this drink, which mixes sweet-and-sour flavors to create the same kind of eye-opening combination as the gas and spark a Zippleback's twin heads produce to create a blast of fire! (Though this smoothie is much safer to drink.)

- 1 cup pineapple juice
- 1 cup orange juice
- 1 cup almond milk
- 1 tablespoon sea buckthorn powder
- 1 frozen banana
- 1 cup frozen mango chunks
- 2 scoops plant-based vanilla protein powder

In a blender, blend the pineapple juice, orange juice, almond milk, sea buckthorn powder, banana, mango, and protein powder until smooth. Divide between two glasses and serve.

DRAGON STATS

BARF AND BELCH

Species: Hideous Zippleback
Class: Mystery
Attack: 12
Speed: 10
Armor: 10
Firepower: 14
Shot Limit: 6
Venom: 0
Jaw Strength: 6 (3x2)
Stealth: 22 (11x2)
Fire: Ammonium nitrate mixed with anhydrous hydrazine

V, GF, DF | Makes 2 drinks

STOICK'S HOMEMADE BUBBLY ALMOST-MEAD

Before we learned to train dragons and Dragon Racing became the coolest way of competing in the whole world, we had tons of ways to compete . . . like sheep counting, sheep lifting, and sheep tossing! And we'd celebrate our winners in Meade Hall, which led to a brand-new competition: mead making! Our great chieftain Stoick won that contest so many times that everyone else went back to lifting sheep. But to this day, we still celebrate wins in Meade Hall with a cup of Stoick's famous recipe!

- ½ cup honey
- ½ cup water
- ¼ teaspoon ground cinnamon
- ½ teaspoon lemon juice
- 2 tablespoons popping candy
- 1½ cups sparkling water or club soda
- 2 lemon slices, for garnish

In a small saucepan over low heat, heat the honey, water, cinnamon, and lemon juice until the honey is dissolved. Remove from the heat and bring to room temperature.

Meanwhile, dip the rims of two glasses in water, then popping candy to coat. Divide the honey mixture and sparkling water or club soda between them and add ice to fill the glasses. Garnish with the lemon slices and serve.

CHAPTER SIX | DESSERTS

A NOTE FROM THE CHIEF ON DESSERTS

Not too long ago, we Berkians lived very different lives. We were in constant conflict with dragons, and surviving was stressful. Even the weather used to be worse!

But what you gotta do when things get hard is look for the joy you can. And one of our greatest joys comes from dessert. A little bit of sweetness at the end of a long, hard day works wonders.

We have cakes that celebrate the Northern Lights (page 118) and ceremonial delights such as Gothi's Crest Cookies (page 128) waiting for us after we've cleaned our supper plates.

And you know what? When the dragons joined us and the stress eased, dessert didn't go away . . . it got better! We had more joy! More to celebrate! And more inspiration for sweet treats, like Cloudjumper's Dragon-Wing Lefse (page 133) or Raincutter's Claws (page 134).

So, finish your peas and get to the treats—I'll race you to it!

—Hiccup Horrendous Haddock III

NORTHERN LIGHTS MERINGUE CAKE

The Northern Lights are captivating and as colorful as any dragon. In fact, some legends speculate that the Northern Lights might even be caused by dragons fighting with each other in the distance, with their bright flames lighting up the sky, but investigations continue. And yes, we do have a cake to celebrate the lights of the sky, because there's never a reason to not celebrate something with a good dessert.

CAKE

7 tablespoons unsalted butter, plus more for greasing

⅔ cup sugar

4 egg yolks

1¼ cups all-purpose flour

1 teaspoon baking powder

3 tablespoons whole milk

½ teaspoon almond extract

MERINGUE

4 egg whites

Pinch Diamond Crystal kosher salt

1 cup granulated sugar

Food coloring (your choice of blue, pink, purple, or green to mimic the Northern Lights)

FILLING

Pistachio pudding mix, prepared according to package instructions

TOPPING

Edible shimmer dust in blue, pink, purple, green, and celestial colors

TO MAKE THE CAKE: Preheat the oven to 350°F. Lightly oil a large cake pan (about 11 by 16 inches), line it with parchment paper, and lightly grease the paper, too.

In a large bowl, beat the butter and sugar until light and fluffy. Add the egg yolks, one at a time, until fully incorporated.

In a medium bowl, sift together the flour and baking powder. Add this mixture to the egg mixture a little at a time, alternating with the milk, then stir in the almond extract. Spread the batter into the pan.

TO MAKE THE MERINGUE: In a mixing bowl, beat the egg whites with the salt. Once stiff, gradually add the sugar and continue to beat until stiff peaks form. Separate this mixture into two or three bowls, depending on the colors you choose to work with. Mix the food coloring into the meringue.

Carefully spread the meringue on top of the cake batter and swirl lightly to achieve a look reminiscent of the Northern Lights. Bake for 25 to 30 minutes, until the meringue is dry. Cool in the pan.

Let the cake cool, then cut in half vertically. Place one half on a serving platter. Spread the pistachio pudding over the cake, using enough to add a generous layer without it spilling out the sides. Top with the remaining half of the cake. Sprinkle and decorate with edible shimmer powder to complete the celestial-inspired work of art.

INGERMAN RATING
+9 Sweetness
+7 Juiciness
+10 Creaminess

V | Serves 16

FOR THE DANCING AND THE DREAMING RUSTIC LAYER CAKE WITH CREAM AND BERRIES

This layer cake is the kind that I like to have every year to celebrate the summer solstice! The solstice is such a great time of year—not only are the dragons extra playful and energetic with the warmer weather, but the bees are also doing their thing, and there's so much honey available, we have plenty to add to a cake to help celebrate the day. Don't forget to whip the cream! That's key. (And don't try to speed up the process by flying loop-de-loops on dragonback. That's messy!)

CAKE

Oil, for greasing

6 eggs, separated

1 cup granulated sugar

½ cup cake flour

¼ cup light rye flour

1 teaspoon baking powder

½ cup honey

¼ cup water

1 teaspoon vanilla extract

FILLING

Vanilla pastry cream mix, prepared according to package instructions

¾ cup berry jam

TOPPING

1½ cups whipping cream

2 tablespoons sugar

1 teaspoon vanilla extract

½ pint fresh mixed berries

Preheat the oven to 350°F and grease two 9-inch round springform cake pans.

In a large mixing bowl, beat the egg whites, then gradually add the sugar, continuing to beat until stiff. Beat the egg yolks in another bowl. Gently fold the beaten yolks and the flours and baking powder into the egg whites until fully incorporated. Pour into the pans and bake for about 30 minutes, until a toothpick inserted in the center comes out clean. Let cool in the pans.

In a small saucepan, heat the honey and water over medium heat until the honey dissolves into the water. Stir in vanilla.

To assemble the cake, slice each cake in half horizontally (a long, serrated knife works well for this). Place one on a cake stand and brush with the honey syrup before spreading an even layer of pastry cream over top. Place another layer of the cake on top of this one and brush again with the honey syrup. This time, spread with the jam. Top with another layer of cake, spread with honey syrup, then more custard. Top with the final layer of cake, pouring a generous amount of honey syrup over top.

Finally, whip the cream, sugar, and vanilla in a large bowl until stiff but fluffy, then add a generous mound on top of the cake, followed by a bounty of berries. Serve slices with additional cream and berries.

V, GF*, DF | Serves a crowd

TWELVE DAYS NORTH OF HOPELESSNESS CAKE

For a long time, dragons besieged Berk, and everything seemed hopeless. When we got a break, around Snoggletog, we'd celebrate—and this kransekake was the centerpiece of the celebration. Now that there's peace and the dragons live with us, we celebrate that, and we celebrate more often. (Which is my favorite thing. The only thing I'd rather do than celebrate is discover a new kind of math.) To honor our dragon friends, the rings of this cake are dyed a ton of different colors . . . though, if you're like me, you can narrow the colors down to match your favorite dragon. (I love you, sweet Meatlug.)

DOUGH

1½ pounds almond flour

1½ pounds confectioners' sugar

½ teaspoon freshly ground cardamom

⅛ teaspoon Diamond Crystal kosher salt

5 egg whites

1 teaspoon almond extract

Food coloring in 3 or 4 colors of your choice

Cooking spray or neutral oil, for greasing

Semolina or cornmeal, for dusting (see note)

ICING

4 cups confectioners' sugar

3 tablespoons meringue powder

8 to 9 tablespoons water

1 tablespoon lemon juice

Food coloring (optional)

SPECIAL TOOLS

Electric mixer

Kransekake cake molds

Pastry bag with a small tip

Preheat the oven to 350°F.

TO MAKE THE DOUGH: In a large mixing bowl, combine the almond flour, confectioners' sugar, cardamom, and salt. Add the egg whites and almond extract, mixing (ideally with an electric mixer) until a dough forms. Divide the dough into three or four portions, depending on how many colors you use, and knead the food coloring into each of them.

Prep the molds by spraying them with a cooking spray or brushing with a neutral oil and dusting with semolina.

To form the rings, roll the dough into logs about a finger's thickness and place them in the molds, according to the color pattern of your choice. Bake until light gold, about 10 minutes. Cool before assembly.

TO MAKE THE ICING: In a medium bowl, vigorously beat the confectioners' sugar, meringue powder, water, lemon juice, and food coloring (if using) until smooth and thick. Transfer the mixture to a pastry bag with a small tip inserted.

Starting with the largest ring, pipe a zigzag of icing onto it and then set the next largest ring on top, repeating with the remaining rings.

*NOTE: Easily make this gluten-free by using a gluten-free cornmeal instead of semolina to dust the pans.

V, GF | Serves 4 to 6

PLASMA BLAST CRÈME BRÛLÉE WITH BERRIES

One unique thing about a Night Fury—aside from its retractable teeth—is that it is the only dragon that fires a purplish blast of plasma. Not lava, or steam, or gas, or electricity, or ice, or plain, old-fashioned fire; but plasma. It's super powerful and, if I might say, such a pleasant color. With a little bit of culinary creativity, we can get this crème brûlée to just about the same shade of purple as Toothless's plasma blasts! A quick puff of flame from a mid-size dragon of the Stoker Class variety is about all you need to finish this dessert off, but a small torch will get the same results. Just be careful! Safety is key in all recipes, especially when they involve fire. Be sure to make this recipe with an adult in a ventilated space. Blisters are frustrating!

CUSTARD

2 cups heavy whipping cream

1 teaspoon vanilla extract

5 egg yolks

½ cup granulated sugar

Purple food coloring, for decorating

TOPPING

5 tablespoons granulated sugar

½ tablespoon food-safe potassium chloride (a sodium-free substitute for salt)

1 to 2 tablespoons high-proof vodka or other clear spirit

Fresh berries, for serving

TO MAKE THE CUSTARD: Preheat the oven to 325°F. In a medium saucepan, bring the cream to a simmer over medium heat, whisking occasionally, then remove from the heat and stir in the vanilla.

In a mixing bowl, beat the egg yolks and sugar until light, then pour in 2 tablespoons of the hot cream while beating the eggs, to temper it, then add the eggs to the cream and stir vigorously and thoroughly until smooth. Whisk in the purple food coloring to achieve the depth of color you desire.

Divide the mixture among four (6 ounce) or six (4 ounce) ramekins. Place these ramekins in a rimmed baking dish, which you'll then add water to, coming halfway up the sides of the ramekins.

Bake until the center of the custard is just barely set, about 40 minutes, depending on the shallowness and size of the ramekins. Remove from the oven and cool on a wire rack, then refrigerate until cold. (This can be made in advance up to this point.)

TO MAKE THE TOPPING: In a small bowl, combine the sugar and potassium chloride and evenly scatter about 2 teaspoons over the top of each custard. Sprinkle or spritz alcohol onto the top of each custard—just enough to dampen the topping. Caramelize the topping with a kitchen torch, enjoying a brief showing of purple as the alcohol ignites.

Top with fresh berries.

NIGHT FURY ABILITIES:

Dive-bombing capability
Plasma blasts
Stealth flight
Supersonic speeds
Echolocation

V+*, V, GF*, DF* | Makes about 4 dozen cookies

HIDDEN WORLD COOKIES

The legends say that the dragons have this, like, ancestral island home, a hidden, expansive cave-like world under the sea of never-ending summer where every kind of tree and flower grows and there's enough fish to last them forever. The legends also mention that there are special kinds of flowers that can only grow in the Hidden World. A fun pastime for younger Vikings is to use their imagination to decorate these cookies to look like flowers that would be in the dragons' hidden world. (It's not actually just for children . . . I do this every week.)

½ cup plus 6 tablespoons (1¾ sticks) salted butter, at room temperature (see note)

⅔ cup confectioners' sugar

3½ ounces marzipan

1 teaspoon vanilla extract

2 cups all-purpose flour, plus more for dusting (see note)

1 batch Icing (page 134)

Food coloring

Pearl sugar

Edible glitters

Sprinkles

SPECIAL TOOL

Cookie cutters

Piping bags fitted with a small tip

In a large bowl, beat the butter, sugar, marzipan, and vanilla extract until light and thoroughly mixed. Add the flour and mix, then knead until a dough forms. Divide this into two disks, wrap in plastic, and chill a couple of hours or overnight.

Preheat the oven to 350°F and line two baking sheets with parchment.

Remove one portion of the dough from the refrigerator and roll out about ¼-inch thick on a lightly floured surface. Cut into shapes using cookie cutters of your choice, and place about 1 inch apart on the prepared pans. Repeat until all the dough is used. Bake until set and barely showing a hint of color, 10 to 15 minutes. Cool on a wire rack.

Divide the icing into as many colors as you'd like and mix with food coloring. Transfer into piping bags fitted with a small tip and use this to outline and fill the surface of the cookies in any design you choose. Decorate with pearl sugar, edible glitter, sprinkles, and other ingredients of your choice.

*NOTE: Easily make vegan and dairy-free by using a plant-based butter substitute. Choose a gluten-free flour blend instead of all-purpose flour if necessary.

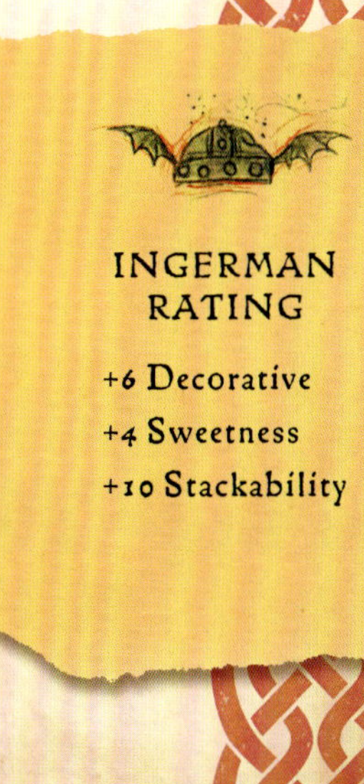

V, DF*, GF* | Makes about 4 dozen cookies

GOTHI'S CREST COOKIES

Hiccup became chieftain of Berk after a massive battle, which had every kind of dragon I'd ever heard of, and at least thirteen different species that I hadn't. It was a big deal all around. But even though Hiccup led Berk to defeat Drago Bludvist and his army, if our village elder, Gothi, had decided he wasn't worthy, Hiccup wouldn't have been accepted as chieftain. Gothi gave him her blessing by marking him with a little bit of soot. It's the same mark you see on these cookies—which you should totally give to someone truly worthy.

- ½ cup plus 6 tablespoons (1¾ sticks) salted butter, at room temperature (see note)
- ¾ cup granulated sugar
- 1½ tablespoons molasses
- 1 teaspoon vanilla extract
- 2 cups all-purpose flour (see note)
- 1 teaspoon baking soda
- 1 egg, beaten
- Coarse sugar, such as demerara, for rolling
- Brown or black icing with a fine tip, for decorating

In a medium bowl, cream the butter and sugar until pale and fluffy, then mix in the molasses and vanilla. Add the flour and baking soda and mix until incorporated. Divide into logs about 1½ inches in diameter, wrap in plastic, and refrigerate a couple of hours or overnight.

Preheat the oven to 350°F. Line your baking sheets with parchment. Brush the logs with the beaten egg, then roll in the coarse sugar. Use a sharp knife to cut the logs into slices about ¼-inch thick. Place these on the baking sheets about an inch and a half apart. Bake until set, about 10 to 12 minutes, then cool on a wire rack.

Use brown or black icing with a fine tip to draw the shape of Gothi's crest on each cookie. See page 151 for a template.

INGERMAN RATING

+3 Regal
+1 Destiny
+7 Pairs with milk

*NOTE: To make gluten-free, use a gluten-free flour blend. Choose a plant-based butter alternative to make dairy-free.

V, GF | Serves 6 to 8

HONEY-VANILLA ICE CREAM

As we all know, not all dragons breathe fire. Some species, most notably the Bewilderbeast, can breathe pure frigidity. This ability to conjure cold has unlocked a whole new kind of snack for us—we call it ice cream. It's cream, right, but it's cold, and more solid than liquid. You add flavoring and toppings (like honey!) and cool down during the three and a half weeks that Berk experiences summertime. The dragon needs to have at least +4 cold ability to properly cool the cream—but be careful! —+7 cold ability and above can make ice cream so cold, you'll get instant brain freeze! We can also make ice cream outdoors during the winter with the chill of the wind, but it's so much easier to get a frost-breathing dragon to help. They're more than happy to chill some ice cream in exchange for a little Dragon Nip!

DRAGON STATS

DRAGO'S BEWILDERBEAST

Species: Bewilderbeast
Class: Tidal
Attack: 50
Speed: 6
Armor: 38
Firepower: 60
Shot Limit: 8
Venom: 0
Jaw Strength: 48
Stealth: 2

ICE CREAM

- 1 vanilla bean
- 2 cups heavy whipping cream
- 1 cup whole milk
- 4 large egg yolks
- ¾ cup granulated sugar
- Pinch Diamond Crystal kosher salt
- ¼ cup honey

MERINGUE

- Cooking spray
- 4 egg whites
- Pinch Diamond Crystal kosher salt
- 1 cup granulated sugar
- ½ teaspoon almond extract
- ½ cup finely chopped almonds
- Edible glitter, for serving

SPECIAL TOOLS

- Ice-cream maker
- Fine-mesh sieve

TO MAKE THE ICE CREAM: Begin by preparing your ice-cream maker according to manufacturer instructions.

Use the tip of a sharp knife to split the vanilla bean lengthwise, then use the back of the knife to scrape out the seeds.

Pour the cream and milk into a medium saucepan and place over medium heat. Scrape in the vanilla bean seeds and pod and heat the liquid until hot and tiny bubbles begin to cling to the sides of the pan, stirring from time to time, about 7 minutes. Remove from the heat and let the vanilla steep.

Meanwhile, in a mixing bowl, whisk the egg yolks and sugar until pale. Stir in the salt.

Temper the eggs by whisking a small amount of cream into them. While continuing to whisk, slowly add the rest of the cream.

Pour this mixture back into the saucepan and cook over low heat, stirring constantly, until thickened to the point of coating the back of a spoon—again, take care not to boil. This should take 5 to 7 minutes. Strain through a fine-mesh sieve into a clean bowl to ensure a smooth, silky ice cream.

Cover the custard with a sheet of plastic wrap and chill at least four hours, or overnight.

Pour into an ice-cream maker and churn according to manufacturer's instructions. When the ice cream reaches a soft-serve consistency, spoon half to an airtight container and drizzle with honey before adding the rest of the ice cream. Swirl the honey throughout using a knife. Freeze until firm.

TO MAKE THE MERINGUE: Preheat the oven to 250°F and line a baking sheet with parchment, then lightly mist with cooking spray. In a mixing bowl, beat the egg whites and salt. Once stiff, gradually add the sugar and continue to beat until stiff peaks form. Fold in the almond extract.

Spread this mixture over the prepared sheet, scatter the almonds on top, and bake until dry, about 1½ hours. When cool enough to handle, break into pieces.

Serve the ice cream with edible glitter and meringue crumbles.

V+*, V, GF*, DF* | Makes about 2 dozen

SNAPTRAPPER-SCENTED CHOCOLATE-BERRY OAT BITES

There are a lot of things to love about being a Viking. Awesome hair, kinship with dragons, oceanfront property, exciting modern food, and of course, discovering new things! One recent example of a discovery: We know that the Snaptrapper dragon can create a sweet-smelling musk to lure unsuspecting prey. Well, we discovered a way to replicate that musk's flavor and turn it into a tasty treat Gobber calls "chocolate," though I don't think the name will stick. But that was only half of the discovery—when you mix chocolate with oats, you get a fantastic blast of sweet flavor that's as good as honey, maybe even better!

1½ cups old-fashioned rolled oats (see note)

⅔ cup confectioners' sugar

¼ cup cocoa powder

¼ cup roughly crumbled freeze-dried berries

⅓ cup salted butter, at room temperature (see note)

½ cup lingonberry preserves

1 teaspoon vanilla extract

Cocoa powder, for rolling

Crushed freeze-dried berries, for rolling

In a large bowl, mix together the oats, sugar, cocoa powder, and freeze-dried berries. Add the butter, lingonberry preserves, and vanilla and stir until coated. Chill for at least 30 minutes, then roll into balls about 1 inch in diameter. Roll in a mix of cocoa powder and crushed freeze-dried berries. Store in the fridge up to a week.

*NOTE: Easily make this vegan, gluten-free, and dairy-free by ensuring the oats are gluten-free and substituting a plant-based butter alternative.

DRAGON STATS

Species: Snaptrapper
Class: Mystery
Attack: 10
Speed: 4
Armor: 4
Firepower: 6
Shot Limit: 4
Venom: 18
Jaw Strength: 28
Stealth: 60

DRAGON STATS
CLOUDJUMPER
Species: Stormcutter
Class: Sharp
Attack: 10
Speed: 17
Armor: 4
Firepower: 12
Shot Limit: 8
Venom: 0
Jaw Strength: 5
Stealth: 30
Fire: Sustained and blazing torus of fire

CLOUDJUMPER'S DRAGON-WING LEFSE

Stormcutters, like Valka's dragon Cloudjumper, are just an absolutely gorgeous example of the variety of dragons. There are two things I love about Stormcutters. First, they have a second set of major wings that gives them an extraordinary amount of control while in flight. The second thing is their personality—you might be surprised to learn that they have some of the warmest, gentlest temperaments to be found among dragons, and they'd much rather be friends than enemies. Being around a Stormcutter feels like being at home in a cozy cottage. Between that and their wafer-thin auxiliary wings, being around one also makes me think of lefse, a cozy snack made from wafer-thin flatbread. You can see how I got there.

LEFSE

2 pounds russet potatoes, peeled and roughly cut into 1-inch pieces

¼ cup (½ stick) unsalted butter

2 tablespoons heavy whipping cream

1 tablespoon granulated sugar

¾ teaspoon Diamond Crystal kosher salt

¾ teaspoon almond extract

1 cup all-purpose flour, plus more for dusting

FILLING

¼ cup (½ stick) salted butter, at room temperature

2 tablespoons granulated sugar

½ tablespoon cinnamon

SPECIAL TOOL

Ricer

TO MAKE THE LEFSE: In a large pot, cook the potatoes in salted, boiling water until tender, about 20 minutes. Then drain and allow to cool a bit before pushing through a ricer. Measure 2 cups and place in a large mixing bowl. (Save any remainders for another use.)

In a small saucepan, melt the butter over medium heat, then stir in the cream, sugar, salt, and almond extract. Pour over the potatoes and mix. Cover and refrigerate for at least several hours.

Add the flour to the potatoes, kneading to thoroughly mix the ingredients and create a smooth, lump-free dough. Divide into balls 1¾ inches in diameter, flatten into pucks, and refrigerate again for 30 minutes or so.

Meanwhile, preheat a large nonstick skillet over medium-low heat. Dust a generous amount of flour over a flat surface (a cloth-covered pastry board is ideal). Rub flour over a rolling pin, too.

Removing a few pucks from the fridge at a time (the dough works best when it remains chilled), dip it into the flour to coat both sides, then place it on the floured board and roll thinly to make a thin circle.

Slide a heatproof spatula under the dough and transfer it to the skillet. Cook for a minute or two until bubbles begin forming on the surface and the underside develops light brown spots, then flip and cook for another minute until the same happens on the other side.

Dust away any excess flour, cover with a clean tea towel, and repeat with the remaining dough.

TO MAKE THE FILLING: In a small bowl, mix together the butter, granulated sugar, and cinnamon. Spread the lefse rounds with this mixture and fold into quarters.

Any unfilled lefse will keep up to a few days in the fridge if folded into quarters and wrapped and sealed in airtight bags.

STORMCUTTER ABILITIES:

X-wing flying

Shooting fire in a spiral shape

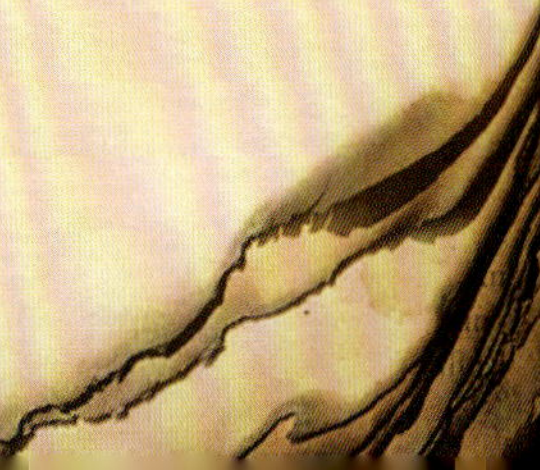

V | Makes 16

RAINCUTTER'S CLAWS

I've heard stories from traveling Vikings about a special kind of pastry named after a bear's claws. Berk has a baked treat that's a lot like that! Ours is a bigger and better pastry than any bearclaw, and we decided to name it after the mighty Raincutter dragon! If you weren't aware, the Raincutter dragon is well-known for its powerful claws—they're twice as long as any bear's, and, though they can be used for defense, they're more often used for playing in the dirt. Raincutters absolutely love to dig . . . almost as much as they love the rain! Speaking of the rain, this pastry is a perfect snack for a rainy day—pair it with a warm cup of Dragon Spit Cider (page 105) and enjoy the gentle pitter-patter of raindrops on your roof!

DOUGH

5 tablespoons salted butter

1 cup whole milk, plus more as needed

1 tablespoon active dry yeast

6 tablespoons granulated sugar, divided

3 cups flour, plus more for dusting

2 tablespoons crumbled freeze-dried berries

2 teaspoons vanilla extract

1 large egg, lightly beaten

FILLING

6 tablespoons salted butter, at room temperature

3 tablespoons packed brown sugar

1 tablespoon cinnamon

2 teaspoons freshly ground cardamom

ICING

1 cup confectioners' sugar

2 tablespoons water

1 tablespoon salted butter, melted

¼ teaspoon vanilla extract

TOPPING

Freeze-dried berries

TO MAKE THE DOUGH: In a medium saucepan, melt the butter over medium-high heat, then add the milk and let it scald. Remove from the heat and cool until lukewarm.

In a large mixing bowl, place the yeast and about half the sugar. Pour a cup or so of the milk over this mixture to cover it and let sit for 5 to 10 minutes until the yeast begins bubbling.

In the meantime, in a separate large bowl, mix the flour, remaining sugar, berries, vanilla, and egg. Add this to the yeast and mix, then turn onto a lightly floured surface and knead for about 10 minutes (use a bench scraper to help with stickiness). (See the instructions in the tip for Meatlug's Sweet Chocolate and Cherry Buns on page 26.) Transfer to a large bowl, cover with a damp tea towel, and let rise until doubled in an area without drafts, about 1 hour.

TO MAKE THE FILLING: Meanwhile, in a small bowl, mix the butter, brown sugar, cinnamon, and cardamom with a fork until combined. Set aside.

On a lightly floured surface, roll out the dough to a rectangle about 16 by 20 inches. Spread the filling over half of it (lengthwise), then fold the dough toward you to form a new rectangle, 8 by 20 inches. Cut the dough into 16 strips. Twist the ends of each in opposite directions two or three times, then roll it around your finger and tuck in the ends.

Place on baking trays lined with parchment paper. Cover again and let rise for another 30 minutes.

Preheat the oven to 400°F. Bake for 10 to 12 minutes, until golden and cooked through.

TO MAKE THE ICING: While the dough is baking, place the confectioners' sugar in a small mixing bowl and gradually add the water, whisking the entire time. Add the butter and vanilla. Drizzle the icing on the twists, then top with freeze-dried berries.

INGERMAN
RATING
-5 Bear
+2 Coziness
+10 Cinnamony

V+, V, GF, DF | Serves 20

RHUBARB-AND-BERRY SOUR CANDIES

I love to have a little snack whenever I'm out on a long flight with Meatlug around Berk and its surrounding islands . . . but most snacks are eaten within a few minutes, and sometimes I want more. The problem with that is you can only carry so many snacks with you, and if your dragon likes to do the occasional loop-de-loop, they might fall away before you even get a chance to eat them! That's where these candies come in—not only can you fit several into your pocket or satchel, but this kind of candy lasts a lot longer than any other snack! (Try one and you'll see!) Plus, the tart flavor is a lot less tempting for your dragon to try to steal away than something like Astrid's Sausage over Sour Cabbage (Surkål) with Mustard (page 79)!

Cooking spray

¾ cup water

2 cups granulated sugar

¾ cup corn syrup

¼ teaspoon citric acid, plus more for coating the candy

1 tablespoon water

½ teaspoon rhubarb-flavored oil

½ teaspoon raspberry-flavored oil

½ teaspoon red food coloring

¼ teaspoon blue food coloring

SPECIAL TOOL

Candy molds

Grease your candy molds with cooking spray.

In a heavy-bottomed saucepan, stir together the water, sugar, and corn syrup and bring to a boil until it reaches the hard ball or hard crack stage at 300°F (this will take about 10 minutes). Remove from the heat and let cool to 225°F.

While you're waiting for the mixture to cool, dissolve the citric acid in the water in a small bowl. When the candy reaches 225°F, add the citric acid mixture, along with the flavored oils and food coloring (start with a few drops of red and add one drop of blue at a time to achieve a berry color).

Pour into the molds and let set for 2 to 3 hours at room temperature. Once they're set but retain some tackiness, remove from the molds and sprinkle more citric acid on the surfaces. Store in an airtight container for up to 2 to 3 months.

V, V+*, DF* | Serves 4

BAKED APPLES WITH RYE AND VANILLA FROZEN YOGURT

On Berk, we totally appreciate contrasts. Dragons, for example, can be the most ferocious fighters you've ever seen—faster and tougher than anything they're up against—and they can also be the sweetest, most devoted friends you've ever had in your life. My sweet Meatlug can cut a boulder in half with a single bite, but she gives the gentlest kisses before she nestles into her bed and goes to sleep for the night. This dessert is just like that—the warm baked apples, with their sweetness and winter spices, contrast so well with the frozen yogurt. It's the perfect mix.

- 4 large apples
- ½ cup all-purpose flour
- ¼ cup rye flour
- ¼ cup brown sugar
- ½ teaspoon cinnamon
- ¼ teaspoon ground cardamom
- ⅛ teaspoon salt
- ¼ cup (½ stick) salted butter (see note)
- ¼ cup chopped sliced almonds
- Vanilla frozen yogurt, for serving (see note)

Preheat the oven to 375°F.

Cut each apple into eight wedges and discard the cores (an apple slicer makes quick work of this). Layer in an 8-by-8-inch baking dish.

In a large bowl, combine the all-purpose flour, rye flour, brown sugar, cinnamon, cardamom, and salt. Cut the butter into the rest of the ingredients. Sprinkle this mixture evenly over the apples. Bake for about 35 minutes, until the apples are tender and the topping golden. (If the topping darkens too quickly, place a sheet of aluminum foil over it midway through baking.)

*NOTE: Make dairy-free and vegan by choosing plant-based alternatives for the butter and frozen yogurt.

GRONCKLE'S HIDDEN ABILITIES:

When Gronckles ingest more than one rock at a time, they will occasionally spit out a brand-new substance in lava form.

V, GF* | Makes about 3 dozen

PEPPARKAKOR FOR SNOGGLETOG

The nice thing about Snoggletog is that it has a ton of old traditions. There is at least one traditional game or meal for every day of the week leading up to Snoggletog, and for days after . . . the only problem is that most of those traditions celebrated hunting and fighting dragons. When the dragons became our friends, we needed some new traditions! One I'd like to suggest is a kinder, gentler dragon hunt . . . we could cut pepparkakor—or cookies—into shapes and decorate them to look like every sort of dragon that we know about and then hide them all over the Great Hall! Kids could hunt the cookies down and share them with their friends! (Or a roaming Hobgobbler . . . they love cookies! Well, they love anything, really . . .)

- ⅔ cup salted butter
- ⅔ cup sugar
- ½ cup molasses
- ¼ cup cream
- 1 teaspoon vanilla extract
- 3 cups flour, plus more for dusting (see note)
- 1 tablespoon ground cinnamon
- 2 teaspoons ground cardamom
- 1½ teaspoons ground ginger
- 1 teaspoon baking soda
- 1 batch Icing (page 122)

SPECIAL TOOLS:

Dragon-shaped cookie cutters

In a small pan, combine the butter, sugar, and molasses over medium-low heat, stirring until the butter melts. Stir in the cream and vanilla and set aside.

In a large bowl, combine the flour, cinnamon, cardamom, ginger, and baking soda. Add the butter mixture and stir to create a dough. Divide and form into two disks, wrap in plastic wrap, and refrigerate for at least 4 hours or overnight.

Preheat the oven to 350°F. Line two baking sheets with parchment paper. Lightly flour a work surface and roll out the dough (working with about a quarter of a disk at a time, keeping the remaining dough chilled until ready to use) until it's about ⅛-inch thick.

Use dragon-shaped cookie cutters to create the shapes of your choice and transfer to the baking sheets. Bake 5 to 7 minutes in the middle of the oven (baking one sheet at a time), until the edges are barely golden. Remove and cool on the baking sheet.

Decorate with icing and store in an airtight container.

*NOTE: To make gluten-free, substitute a gluten-free flour blend.

INGERMAN RATING

+10: Tradition
+6 Hideability
+7 Fun

V | Makes 9

BERK BIRKES

There are no bad desserts. Certainly, there are no bad desserts included in this chronicle . . . but I think the overwhelming favorite among the townsfolk of Berk might be, well, birkes. Is it because the name of this sweet and flaky pastry sounds so much like that of our home island? Or is it just due to a deep, island-wide love of marzipan? I'll have to conduct thorough research to be sure. In the meantime, whip up a batch for yourself and find out why my fellow Vikings are such fans of this terrific treat!

One 14-ounce package frozen puff pastry, defrosted

½ cup (1 stick) butter, at room temperature

7 ounces marzipan

1 cup sugar

1 egg, lightly beaten

Poppy seeds, for topping

Preheat the oven to 350°F. Line a rimmed baking sheet with parchment paper. Roll out the pastry dough into a long, 18-by-12-inch rectangle.

In a small dish, mix the butter, marzipan, and sugar with a fork or your hands until creamy. Spread this mixture in a thin layer along the long edge of the dough, covering about two-thirds of the surface. Fold the dough in thirds, lengthwise, starting with the dough that's covered with the butter, to close the remonce into the dough. Use a sharp knife to cut the dough into 2-inch slices and transfer to the baking sheet.

Brush the beaten egg over the top of each pastry and sprinkle with poppy seeds. Bake until golden brown, 15 to 20 minutes. Let cool on the baking sheet.

V, DF* | Makes one 8-inch cake

SKILLET APPLE CAKE

If you don't bake all your apples to pair with frozen yogurt (Baked Apples with Rye and Vanilla Frozen Yogurt, page 139), then might I suggest this amazing skillet cake? A good cast-iron pan is needed (Oh! Don't forget to season the pan—oil with a high smoke point and a quick puff of fire from any dragon should help with that) and then you're off to the Dragon Races! This is another cozy dessert meant to be enjoyed on a chilly day in front of a fire with a good book and your favorite dragon napping (snoring!) by your side. Doesn't that sound wonderful? It so is.

1 cup (2 sticks) butter, at room temperature, plus more for greasing (see note)

1¾ cups all-purpose flour

¼ cup rye flour

2 teaspoons baking powder

½ teaspoon cinnamon, plus more for dusting

½ teaspoon cardamom

¼ teaspoon Diamond Crystal kosher salt

¾ cup granulated sugar

2 eggs

2 teaspoons vanilla extract

2 or 3 large apples, peeled and thinly sliced

¼ cup brown sugar, for dusting

Preheat the oven to 350°F and grease an 8-inch cast-iron pan with butter.

In a medium mixing bowl, combine the all-purpose flour, rye flour, baking powder, cinnamon, cardamom, and salt. Set aside. Using a stand mixer (a hand mixer will do in a pinch), cream the butter and sugar until pale, about 3 minutes. Add the eggs and vanilla, mixing well. Add the flour mixture and stir to incorporate. Pour the batter into the pan. Arrange the apple slices on top, in a circular shape. Dust cinnamon and brown sugar over the top. Bake for about an hour, until a toothpick inserted in the center comes out clean. (If the top browns too quickly, place a sheet of foil over the top while baking). Let cool for about 30 minutes and serve warm.

*NOTE: To make this dairy-free, simply substitute a plant-based butter alternative for the butter.

DIETARY CONSIDERATIONS

V+ = Vegan | V+* = Can be easily made Vegan
V = Vegetarian | V* = Can be easily made Vegetarian
GF = Gluten-free | GF* = Can be easily made Gluten-free
DF = Dairy-free | DF* = Can be easily made Dairy-free

Hiccup's Harmless Porridge with Berries and Butter **V, V+*, DF*, GF***

Ruffnut and Tuffnut's Nutty Granola with Skyr, Two Ways **V+*, V, GF, DF***

Sveler Shields **V**

Toothless's Treat Waffles **V**

Meatlug's Sweet Chocolate and Cherry Buns V

Tuffnut's Braided Beard Bread **V, V+*, DF***

Fire and Honey Bacon **GF, DF**

Chieftain's Cheese Pie (for Stoick the Vast) **V, GF***

Pyttipanna (Leftover Hash) Sweet Potato Hash and Fried Eggs **GF, DF**

Berkian Creamy Cod and Potato Stew **GF**

Hobgobbler's Favorite Yellow Pea and Ham Stew with Homemade Croutons **V*, GF*, DF**

Snotlout's Burned Snout Soup **GF*, DF***

Gobber's Homemade Yak Noodle Soup **GF*, DF***

Gothi's Creamy Potato Salad with Herbs **V, GF**

Valka's Creamy Cucumber and Fennel Salad with Skyr and Dill **V, GF**

Stormfly Slaw **V, GF**

Nordic Harvest Salad **V+*, V, GF*, DF**

Horseradish Crème **V, GF***

Horseradish Dill Crème Fraîche **V, GF**

Wild Berry BBQ Sauce **V, GF*, DF**

Calabrian Chimi **V, GF, DF**

Dill Fennel Chimi **V+, V, GF, DF**

Raincutter's Rugbrød and Grubs **V**

Hiccup's t Bites with Cheese and Cured Meat **GF**

Isle of Gravlax **GF, DF**

Honey- and Lingonberry-Roasted Carrots **V, GF, DF**

Zesty Cipollini Onions **V+, V, GF, DF**

Balsamic Mushrooms **V+, V, GF, DF**

Sweet Potato Hash **V, V+*, GF**

Potatoes with Charred Herbs **V, GF**

Gothi's Cabbage and Barley with Honey- and Lingonberry-Glazed Vegetables and Herbs **V, DF**

Gobber the Belch's Roast Chicken with Beets and BBQ Sauce **GF, DF**

Astrid's Sausage over Sour Cabbage (Surkål) with Mustard **V+*, V*, GF, DF***

Spitfyre Steak Bowl **GF**

Dragon Fire Chicken Spire

Gobber the Belch's Roasted Turkey Wings **GF***

Stoick's Rustic Baked Meatballs with Honey Gravy and Geitost **GF***

Stoick's Roast Pork with Vinegary Red Cabbage (Rødkål) and Apples **GF, DF***

Flaky Pan-Seared Cod with Potatoes, Creamed Greens, and Dill **GF**

Hiccup's Creamy Dill-Poached Haddock with New Potatoes **GF**

Terrible Terror's Dilled Prawns **GF*, DF***

Fishlegs's Fish Sticks with New Potatoes and Dill **GF***

Hiccup's Salmon with Potatoes **GF**

Whole Salt-Crust Roasted Fish **GF, DF**

Astrid's Yaknog **V, GF**

Dragon Spit Cider **V, V+, GF, DF**

Hiccup and Toothless's Smoky Strawberry Black Tea Blend **V, V+, GF, DF**

Bewilderbeast's Icy Skyr **V, GF**

Gløgg for Snoggletog **V, V+, GF, DF**

Barf and Belch's Sweet-and-Sour Sea Buckthorn Smoothie **V, V+, GF, DF**

Stoick's Homemade Bubbly Almost-Mead **V, GF, DF**

Northern Lights Meringue Cake **V**

For the Dancing and the Dreaming Rustic Layer Cake with Cream and Berries **V**

Twelve Days North of Hopelessness Cake **V, GF*, DF**

Plasma Blast Crème Brûlée with Berries **V, GF**

Hidden World Cookies **V, V+*, GF*, DF***

Gothi's Crest Cookies **V, DF*, GF***

Honey-Vanilla Ice Cream **V, GF**

Snaptrapper-Scented Chocolate-Berry Oat Bites **V+*, V, GF*, DF***

Cloudjumper's Dragon-Wing Lefse **V***

Raincutter's Claws **V**

Rhubarb-and-Berry Sour Candies **V+, V, GF, DF**

Baked Apples with Rye and Vanilla Frozen Yogurt **V, V+*, DF***

Pepparkakor for Snoggletog **V, GF***

Berk Birkes **V, V+*, DF***

Skillet Apple Cake **V, DF***

MEASUREMENT CONVERSIONS

VOLUME

Cup	Tablespoons	Teaspoons	Fluid Ounces
1/16 cup	1 tablespoon	3 teaspoon	½ fluid ounce
⅛ cup	2 tablespoons	6 teaspoons	1 fluid ounce
¼ cup	4 tablespoons	12 teaspoons	2 fluid ounces
⅓ cup	5⅓ tablespoons	16 teaspoons	2⅔ fluid ounces
½ cup	8 tablespoons	24 teaspoons	4 fluid ounces
⅔ cup	10⅔ tablespoons	32 teaspoons	5⅓ fluid ounces
¾ cup	12 tablespoons	36 teaspoons	6 fluid ounces
1 cup	16 tablespoons	48 teaspoons	8 fluid ounces

Gallon	Quart	Pint	Cup	Fluid Ounces
1/16 gallon	¼ quart	½ pint	1 cup	8 fluid ounces
⅛ gallon	½ quart	1 pint	2 cups	16 fluid ounces
¼ gallon	1 quart	2 pint	4 cup	32 fluid ounces
½ gallon	2 quarts	4 pint	8 cups	64 fluid ounces
1 gallon	4 quarts	8 pint	16 cups	128 fluid ounces

TEMPERATURES

Fahrenheit	Celsius
200°	93°
225°	107°
250°	121°
275°	135°
300°	149°
325°	163°
350°	177°
375°	191°
400°	204°
425°	218°
450°	232°

WEIGHTS

Ounces	Grams
½ ounce	14 grams
1 ounce	28 grams
2 ounces	57 grams
3 ounces	85 grams
4 ounces	113 grams
5 ounces	142 grams
6 ounces	170 grams
10 ounces	283 grams
14 ounces	397 grams
16 ounces	454 grams
32 ounces	907 grams

LENGTH

Imperial	Metric
1 inch	2½ centimeters
2 inches	5 centimeters
4 inches	10 centimeters
6 inches	15 centimeters
8 inches	20 centimeters
10 inches	25 centimeters
12 inches	30 centimeters

TEMPLATES

SVELER SHIELDS

GOTHI'S CREST COOKIES

ABOUT THE AUTHORS

DAYTONA DANIELSEN is an author whose fiction and food writing evoke the forest, fjords, and folklore of her Norwegian heritage. Her cookbooks, including *Modern Scandinavian Baking* and *Disney Frozen: The Official Cookbook*, celebrate Nordic flavors and traditions, whereas her novels and short stories weave together the myths, mysteries, and haunting beauty of the north. She holds an MFA in fiction from Pacific University and lives near Seattle, Washington, with her two children. Find more at her website, daytonadanielsen.com.

ERIK BURNHAM is lost somewhere in the north woods of Minnesota, writing novels, making comics, learning the baritone ukulele, and leaning as far into creative things as he can. His Scandinavian ancestors come from Værøy in the Lofoten Islands, where rumor has it the locals were known for catching eagles with their bare hands. Erik, on the other hand, has pinched a nerve putting on a T-shirt. (That's a net loss for evolution, but still impressive in its own way.) You can find him online at www.burnhamania.com.

ACKNOWLEDGMENTS

Vincent and Audrey, somehow I blinked, and I no longer have little children, but rather a preteen and a teenager. I remember watching the *How to Train Your Dragon* movies with you when you were small, never imagining that one day we'd work together to create a book of recipes fit for a Viking-esque crew. Though you've been part of the creation of all my cookbooks (you're the best taste-testers I could ask for), you've especially left your mark on this one with your contributions.

Audrey, your recipe concepts brought both authenticity and whimsy to so many of these dishes, including Twelve Days North of Hopelessness Cake, Toothless's Treat Waffles, Cloudjumper's Dragon-Wing Lefse, Raincutter's Claws, and Northern Lights Meringue Cake. Vincent, your scientific curiosity and experimentation elevated these recipes (especially the Plasma Blast Crème Brûlée with Berries and Barf and Belch's Sweet-and-Sour Sea Buckthorn Smoothie) to a true dragon-approved level. (Who knew one could create purple flames from edible ingredients?) It has been an absolute joy to create this with you.

DAYTONA DANIELSEN

I'd like to thank editor Sami Alvarado for inviting me to play in a whole new sandbox and Daytona Danielsen for the fun collaboration. Many thanks also to the fine folks at Universal and the many creatives who have contributed to the *How to Train Your Dragon* franchise over the years. I'd also like to single out my sister-in-law Jill; I'm sorry you're gone. I would've loved to have seen your reaction to the puns. This one's for you.

ERIK BURNHAM

ACKNOWLEDGMENTS

We'd like to thank our partners at NBCUniversal and Universal Epic Universe for their contributions to this book:

Mike Sund
Barb Layman
Kelsey Parrotte
Michael Vollman
Scott Seiffert
Alyssa Cardenas
Shreya Tatkar
Natalie Hyman
Jen Ockelmann-Wagner
Danny Evanilla
Christopher Colón
Robert Martinez Jr.
Jens Dahlmann
Tosh Benson
Matt Heiden
Vikki Eichner
Megan Startz
Jannine Beier

INDEX

D

F

G

PO Box 3088
San Rafael, CA 94912
www.insighteditions.com

Find us on Facebook: www.facebook.com/InsightEditions
Follow us on Instagram: @insighteditions

ISBN: 979-8-3374-0073-0

Publisher: Raoul Goff
SVP, Group Publisher: Vanessa Lopez
VP, Creative: Chrissy Kwasnik
VP, Manufacturing: Alix Nicholaeff
Editorial Director: Thom O'Hearn
Art Director: Stuart Smith
Designer: Brooke McCullum
Associate Editor: Sami Alvarado
Managing Editor: Shannon Ballesteros
Production Manager: Deena Hashem
Strategic Production Planner: Lina s Palma-Temena

Photography by Waterbury Publications
Food Stylist: Josh Hake

Insight Editions, in association with Roots of Peace, will plant two trees for each tree used in the manufacturing of this book. Roots of Peace is an internationally renowned humanitarian organization dedicated to eradicating land mines worldwide and converting war-torn lands into productive farms and wildlife habitats. Roots of Peace will plant two million fruit and nut trees in Afghanistan and provide farmers there with the skills and support necessary for sustainable land use.

Manufactured in China by Insight Editions

10 9 8 7 6 5 4 3 2 1